GEORGIA'S EMERGING ECOSYSTEM FOR TECHNOLOGY STARTUPS

Nino Nanitashvili and Paul Vandenberg

MARCH 2023

Country Report No. 6
Ecosystems for Technology Startups in Asia and the Pacific

ASIAN DEVELOPMENT BANK

© 2023 Asian Development Bank
6 ADB Avenue, Mandaluyong City, 1550 Metro Manila, Philippines
Tel +63 2 8632 4444; Fax +63 2 8636 2444
www.adb.org

Some rights reserved. Published in 2023.

ISBN 978-92-9270-036-2 (print); 978-92-9270-037-9 (electronic); 978-92-9270-038-6 (ebook)
Publication Stock No. TCS230045-2
DOI: http://dx.doi.org/10.22617/TCS230045-2

The views expressed in this publication are those of the authors and do not necessarily reflect the views and policies of the Asian Development Bank (ADB) or its Board of Governors or the governments they represent.

ADB does not guarantee the accuracy of the data included in this publication and accepts no responsibility for any consequence of their use. The mention of specific companies or products of manufacturers does not imply that they are endorsed or recommended by ADB in preference to others of a similar nature that are not mentioned.

By making any designation of or reference to a particular territory or geographic area, or by using the term "country" in this document, ADB does not intend to make any judgments as to the legal or other status of any territory or area.

Please contact pubsmarketing@adb.org if you have questions or comments with respect to content, or if you wish to obtain copyright permission for your intended use that does not fall within these terms, or for permission to use the ADB logo.

Corrigenda to ADB publications may be found at http://www.adb.org/publications/corrigenda.

Note:
In this publication, "$" refers to United States dollars.

All photos are owned by ADB unless otherwise stated.

Cover design by Joe Mark Ganaban.

Contents

Tables and Figure

Foreword

Business models continue to evolve rapidly, spurred by new digital technologies and their deployment in providing goods and services in innovative ways. We can now order food, hail a taxi, move money, arrange travel, watch entertainment, shop for just about anything, and even take courses or consult a doctor using digital methods. At a deeper and often less visible level, technology is affecting production processes in the form of Industry 4.0. Technology-based startup enterprises—or tech startups, for short—are an important part of the evolving business-to-business and business-to-consumer landscape in Asia and the Pacific as well as globally.

Startups develop in an ecosystem that can support—or hinder—their development. That ecosystem involves many national elements, but regional and international factors also are important, especially in increasingly open and globalized economies. Finance, often from venture capital, and skilled personnel, including both tech experts and entrepreneurs, are important parts of the ecosystem. Good digital infrastructure and supportive government policy are also critical. Startups develop best when the markets for their goods and services are large and active.

This report analyzes Georgia's ecosystem and assesses the extent to which it is supportive of the growing number of startups. The report focuses on startups in four areas: agritech, edtech, healthtech, and greentech (also known as cleantech). These four areas not only contribute to economic activity but can have a deeper impact on socioeconomic development. Edtech and healthtech contribute to human capital formation while agritech improves productivity and raises incomes in the rural sector where many of the poor work. Greentech advances environmental sustainability and climate change mitigation.

This analysis of the startup ecosystem provides recommendations for policy makers in Georgia, the Caucasus, and other regions. My hope is that improved ecosystems can better support startups throughout the Asia and Pacific region.

Albert Park
Chief Economist
Asian Development Bank

Acknowledgments

This report was written by Nino Nanitashvili, a consultant, and Paul Vandenberg of the Asian Development Bank (ADB). Aimee Hampel-Milagrosa provided guidance on study design, reviewed several drafts of the report, and provided invaluable comments. Rana Hasan and Lei Lei Song offered management support.

ADB's Georgia Resident Mission reviewed the report and helped solicit comments from the Government of Georgia. The authors would like to thank key experts from government, incubators, accelerators, development partners, investors, academic institutions, and startups who provided invaluable insights to the researcher that were used in the preparation of this study. The draft report was reviewed by Georgia's Innovation and Technology Agency.

Tuesday Soriano copyedited the report, Joe Mark Ganaban provided layout services, and Amanda Isabel Mamon provided administrative support, contracting, and manuscript management.

Abbreviations

ADB	Asian Development Bank
AI	artificial intelligence
B2B	business to business
EBRD	European Bank for Reconstruction and Development
EFSE	European Fund for Southeast Europe
EU	European Union
FTA	free trade agreement
GDP	gross domestic product
GENIE	Georgia National Innovation Ecosystem project
GITA	Georgia's Innovation and Technology Agency
GVCA	Georgian Venture Capital Association
HCI	Human Capital Index
ICT	information and communication technology
IT	information technology
PRC	People's Republic of China
R&D	research and development
SaaS	Software as a Service
SMEs	small and medium-sized enterprises
SPV	special purpose vehicle
STEM	science, technology, engineering, and mathematics
UNDP	United Nations Development Programme
US	United States
USAID	United States Agency for International Development
VAT	value-added tax
VC	venture capital

Executive Summary

Technology-based startups are an important form of business organization around the world. They are driven by innovation and entrepreneurship, and many develop into large high-tech firms that can dominate the economy. Fostering more successful startups will help expand and modernize the economy of Georgia. A startup can be defined as a business that develops new technologies or utilizes existing technologies to produce innovative products and services that target a market need or problem, can generate profits, and develop a business model that is scalable.

Startups are emerging in sectors that promote development, such as education, health, agriculture, and the green economy. However, e-commerce, fintech, artificial intelligence, and digital platforms remain the most common tech startup sectors in Georgia. Agritech startups can help farmers, including those who are poor, increase efficiency and yields and improve market linkages. Cleantech startups that use green technology solutions can help reduce environmental damage, support climate change adaptation, and decrease energy consumption. Edtech startups use technology to improve teaching and learning. Healthtech encompasses innovations in medical products, digital solutions for managing healthcare systems, and solutions for improving patient diagnosis and treatment. These four sectors are the focus of this report.

The views of stakeholders and startups are important for ideas on how to improve the ecosystem. The study draws on interviews with a range of ecosystem stakeholders and startup entrepreneurs. Stakeholders included government officials, managers of incubators and accelerators, and experts at financial institutions. The Georgian startups selected for consultation were operating in one of the four sectors and provided valuable insights into the key obstacles they face.

Ranking

Georgia is ranked 80th out of 100 countries in the Global Startup Ecosystem Index. The ranking is based on the quantity and quality of startups and the business environment. Among the cited drawbacks of the country's ecosystem are a lack of experienced entrepreneurs, limited private investment capital, and a small market (population 3.7 million).

Georgia ranks seventh among 190 countries in the Ease of Doing Business Index. The country also ranks 12th globally and seventh in Europe on the Index of Economic Freedom. With an overall score above regional and global averages, the country outperforms its peers in both trade and business freedom, according to the Heritage Foundation. The overall business climate in Georgia is attractive to entrepreneurs, as business registration can be completed in less than 30 minutes, and startup founders noted the ease of streamlined tax procedures through the Revenue Service Agency's digitized platform. Senior managers in Georgia spend significantly less time on regulatory compliance than in other countries in Europe and Central Asia or in upper middle-income countries.

Innovation, Research, and Market Analysis

Local businesses need to focus more on innovation. Weaknesses that hinder the success of a more vibrant startup community include limited innovation capacity, a lack of entrepreneurial culture, low growth of innovative companies, and limited availability of venture capital.

Research and development are limited. Gross expenditure on research has increased in recent years, but remains far below the European Union (EU) target of 3% of gross domestic product (GDP). Companies invest little in innovation, collaboration between scientists and industry is limited, and research institutions need improvement. Universities can apply for research grants through the government's Shota Rustaveli National Science Foundation, but the amount of funding is limited and conditional. The Knowledge Transfer and Innovation Center at Ivane Javakhishvili Tbilisi State University has been working on the commercialization of science, but no significant results have been achieved.

In Georgia, it is not common to conduct thorough market research to determine demand for a product. Startups generally use national statistics or data on what is happening outside Georgia in certain sectors and often lack a good understanding of the local market. The availability of detailed, industry-specific reports and data on Georgia was cited as a challenge by startups. Where reports and data do exist, startups lack expertise in how to find them (including for the international market).

Digital uptake is high in Georgia compared with neighboring countries and those at the same income level. This increases the market for startups because their products and services have digital elements. However, there is still a noteworthy digital divide between urban and rural areas, as well as socioeconomic differences. The potential of digitalization is not fully utilized by businesses, especially small and medium-sized enterprises (SMEs) outside Tbilisi. There is also a significant gap in digital skills among the population, with lower skills in peripheral areas.

Talent

Human capital is at the heart of the startup ecosystem. Tech talent and entrepreneurs who are competent, courageous, and have a business mindset are key assets to this system. Creating a startup requires a combination of skill, passion, and risk-taking. Georgia has a relatively short history of free markets and a shallow entrepreneurship culture. Georgia has recently made tremendous improvements in education participation and learning outcomes. Nearly a decade ago, the country introduced comprehensive reforms at all levels of education with the goal of creating a credible education system that would enable learning according to international standards. Substantial funding from international donors has been allocated to ongoing education reforms. Public spending on education has been increased to 3.9% of GDP in 2020, slightly below the EU average of 4.6% in 2018.

Government Support

Government support for startups is focused on three areas. These are digital training, technology parks and innovation centers (i.e., infrastructure), and grants for early-stage startups. This support is provided to all startups and businesses, so there are no specific policies, programs, or incentives for startups in agritech, cleantech, edtech, and healthtech.

Startups are looking for tax incentives. The startups interviewed indicated that there are no specific tax exemptions or incentives for startups. Startups are not registered as a different legal entity than other small, medium-sized, or large enterprises. Rather, all registered startups are considered limited liability companies and must comply with standard tax requirements. Most taxes relevant to businesses are 20% personal income tax, 4% pension contribution, 15% corporate tax (profit), and 18% value-added tax (VAT). Startups can benefit from a reduction of these tax rates.

Higher thresholds for import tax (tariff) exemptions would help startups, especially manufacturers. The rates for imported goods are 0%, 5%, and 12%, depending on the type of project. Import taxes are relevant for hardware-based technology startups that depend on component and material imports from abroad. Imported products worth more than $90 (GEL300) are subject to import tax. Removing or raising the threshold on prototype components would benefit early-stage hardware-based startups.

The virtual economic zone for information technology services companies is not well known. Enterprises joining this zone do not pay VAT or profit tax. Over 10 years, more than 1,000 companies have registered for zone status, but none of the startups interviewed knew about it or the tax benefits.

Finance

The grant program of Georgia's Innovation and Technology Agency (GITA) is a major stimulator for startups in the creation and post-prototyping stages. The program targets first-time entrepreneurs who are not required to have a registered legal entity. The grants help entrepreneurs avoid risk (since they are not loans or equity), while providing cash flow that can be used to attract tech talent or pay for marketing costs. In addition to finance, GITA provides mentoring, training, access to Silicon Valley experts and a panel of judges, and networking with other local startups. The best-performing startups funded by GITA are introduced to potential partners and investors, including through trips to the United States.

Some entrepreneurs view grants as an end in themselves rather than a means. Their focus on obtaining grants diverts their attention from validating the product and business model in the marketplace with consumers (and not just the grant competition judges). The judges may be less critical than investors seeking a return on investment. Startups that focus only on winning grants become serial grant applicants that fail to gain traction with consumers and investors to become sustainable.

Bank loans are not a common source of capital for technology startups. Banks view startups as risky and uncertain ventures. It is difficult for startups to service loans regularly (i.e., monthly or quarterly) because they have little or no revenue in the early stages. Collateral is difficult to provide given the intangibility of technology products.

Lending supports SMEs—but not specifically tech startups. Georgia's banking and microcredit sector has special lending programs tailored to small businesses and startups, however, the latter are often defined as any new business.

For example, TBC Bank has launched Startuperi, which is available to all SMEs and offers credit as well as training, business networking meetings, and workshops. The bank provides startup loans with the need to pledge collateral. This approach of considering every new business as a startup is also followed by other financial institutions in the country. They treat startups the same as other SMEs and do not have specific programs for enterprises developing software, hardware, or other tech-related solutions. The Female Start Upper program is also not focused on technology. One exception is InnovFin, an initiative of the European Investment Bank and the European Commission, which supports projects that are riskier and difficult to assess, and therefore often have difficulty accessing funding.

Few credit programs target startups in agritech, cleantech, edtech, and healthtech. However, startups in these sectors can apply and gain access. Access is more likely at the growth stage when there is already a product or service on the market. From the interviews, it appears that most startups have little knowledge or understanding of funding options from financial institutions.

The venture capital market in Georgia is at an early stage of development. However, several groups have emerged recently to promote venture capital and build a network of angel investors. Investment has been supported by the Law on Promotion and Guarantees of Investment Activity (2006) and the Law on Investment of Funds (2020) (Legislative Herald of Georgia 2020). The laws provide the regulatory framework for globally integrated portfolio investments, i.e., capital markets that can provide Georgian businesses with diversified sources of capital from home and abroad. This will promote Georgia's economic growth in two ways: it will make it easier for Georgian investors to trade in foreign markets, and it will give Georgian businesses access to international capital to expand their businesses.

Angel investors have also emerged as a source of funding for startups. Some are organized into networks. For example, Axel is a network of angel investors that brings together investors from Georgia and the Baltic countries. It organizes meetings where selected startups can pitch and share ideas. Few investments have yet to be made.

Investment funds and special purpose vehicles (SPVs) are emerging as investment tools. Both are a means of pooling investor funds. While an SPV invests in a single company, a fund invests in multiple companies. In Georgia, SPVs do not have a specific or special legal form. According to the Law on Investment of Funds, a fund may be established as a joint stock company. A closed-end registered investment company may also be registered as a limited liability company or a limited partnership. Under this law, a registered investment fund may have no more than 20 retail investors, while an authorized investment fund may have more than 20.

None of the investor groups has a specific focus on agritech, edtech, cleantech, or healthtech. However, startups in all four areas may pursue funding options with these stakeholders. None of the startups interviewed for this study has approached a domestic investment fund or angel investor. Investments by existing venture capital firms in clean energy, agriculture, or healthcare tend to go to large businesses, rather than to startups. However, large venture capital firms view supporting education and the environment as part of their corporate social responsibility—a characteristic that startups seeking funds could use to their advantage. This development could lead to impact investing, which is not yet practiced in Georgia.

Incubators and Accelerators

Incubators and accelerator programs are still relatively new in Georgia. Of the startups interviewed, only a few had participated in them. Those that had participated emphasized that they had a significant impact on product and customer development and contact with potential partners and investors. They helped founders improve their understanding of how to run a startup, including aspects of fundraising. This sentiment was also expressed for programs that did not provide grants or equity investments, but helped founders tap into investor networks through demo days and other means. The sample size of these interviews is too small to draw generalized conclusions, but they do suggest a pattern: startups that received structured and longer training and mentoring made significant progress in product development and market validation.

Many incubators are one-off projects that are not sustained. A major reason for these ad hoc projects is the lack of access to stable and sustainable funding and a reliance on donor funding for initiatives of short duration. For each iteration, they must go through a fundraising process and convince stakeholders, which takes time and effort and can curb enthusiasm. Incubator and accelerator managers struggle to find a profitable business model to operate. None of the programs charge participation fees and providing a share of equity to the program is rarely a requirement for a participating startup. Even if an incubator asks a startup to give up some equity in exchange for incubation services (e.g., Redberry Startup Studio), that equity cannot be easily liquidated and used to cover the incubator's operating costs. For incubator or accelerator programs to become self-sustaining, they should consider revenue-generating mechanisms such as charging fees.

Introduction

Georgia's technology startup scene has shown promising growth since 2015. The enthusiasm of young entrepreneurs, coupled with supportive government programs, local and nonprofit initiatives, and international donor funding, is creating momentum for technology-based startup enterprises (tech startups) to flourish. The most common sectors in which startups have emerged in Georgia are e-commerce, fintech, artificial intelligence (AI), and digital information-based service platforms. The emergence of startups in development-oriented sectors, such as education, health, agriculture, and the green economy, is happening but at a slower pace.

This report analyzes the startup ecosystem in Georgia by defining the pillars and players of the ecosystem, as well as the current support mechanisms, and identifying opportunities for its further development. The analysis focuses on the existing conditions and prospects for startups to thrive in four specific areas: agritech, cleantech, edtech, and healthtech.

These four sectors hold considerable promise for social and environmental progress and economic growth. Agritech startups help farmers, including those who are poor, to increase efficiency and yields, improve market linkages, and engage in sustainable farming. Startups that use green technology solutions—in other words, cleantech— reduce environmental damage, support climate change adaptation, and decrease energy consumption. Education technology startups use technology to improve teaching and learning processes and outcomes, both inside and outside the classroom. Healthtech encompasses technological innovation by developing innovative medical products, providing digital solutions to manage healthcare systems, and improving patient diagnosis and treatment.

Digitalization is becoming a key competitive advantage and growth driver both within economies and globally. Demand for technological solutions that benefit society and the economy is increasing as people become more tech-savvy and more processes rely on technology. Startups that take advantage of this opportunity and offer efficient solutions for sustainable development are receiving significant attention. Accordingly, this report analyzes the prospects for Georgia in these four areas (agritech, cleantech, edtech, and healthtech) and the ecosystem that supports them.

Methodology

To gain meaningful insights, interviews were conducted with 14 ecosystem stakeholders (Appendix 1) and 23 tech startup founders (Appendix 2), all from Georgia. Stakeholders included government officials, managers of incubators and accelerators, and staff of financial institutions and educational institutions. Startups were selected based on their presence in the four sectors through word of mouth and referrals from stakeholders. The interviews and other research were mostly conducted in 2021 and early 2022. The startups sector changes rapidly and any new developments may not be captured in the report. Therefore, the report is based on qualitative analysis (from interviews and documents) and not a quantitative survey of startups. The latter would not have been practical or reliable given the small number of actual bona fide startups in the four selected sectors.

Although there are different definitions of a startup depending on the country, culture, and environment, this report defines a startup as a business that develops new technologies or utilizes existing technologies to produce innovative products and services that address a market need or problem, can generate profits, and are scalable.

This report also incorporates information, insights, and observations from other existing reports and studies. Data were obtained from statistical sources and referenced.

The report has three main sections. The first is this introduction. The second section examines the characteristics of Georgia's ecosystem and its stakeholders, and explores the challenges and opportunities faced by the startups, in part through interviews with enterprises from the four target sectors. The third section provides recommendations to foster the development of Georgia's startup ecosystem.

Overview of Georgia's Technology Ecosystem

Startups emerge and perform well under certain conditions. Like living organisms, they need a suitable environment to grow and develop. The ecosystem for startups is composed of many actors, institutions, and relationships (see figure). The more interconnected and complementary the ecosystem, the greater the chances that the startup community will thrive. An ecosystem includes digital infrastructure, government policies, access to funding, human capital, workspaces, organizations such as incubators and accelerators, and a culture that encourages entrepreneurship and innovation.

Startup Ecosystem Map

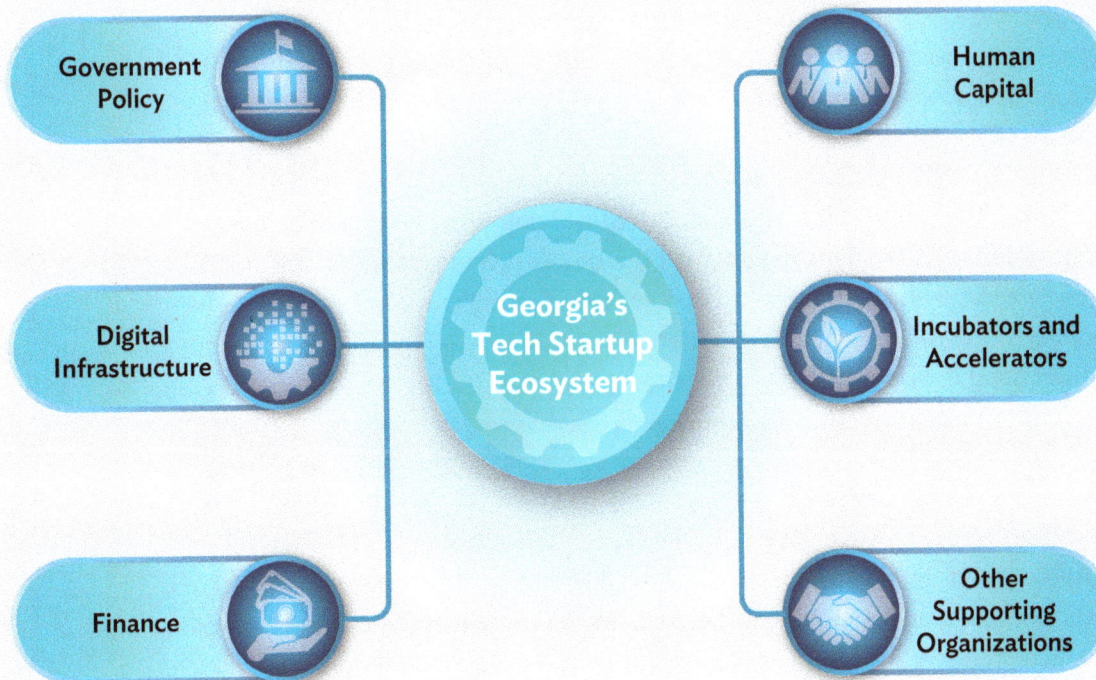

Government Policy — Human Capital — Digital Infrastructure — Georgia's Tech Startup Ecosystem — Incubators and Accelerators — Finance — Other Supporting Organizations

Source: Authors.

With an emerging information and communication technology (ICT) sector, Georgia is working hard to establish itself as a growing hub for information and communication technology. Since the creation of Georgia's Innovation and Technology Agency in 2014, significant efforts have been made to develop the digital ecosystem in Georgia, from improving physical infrastructure, including broadband connectivity, tech parks, and innovation centers, to providing grants to startups and offering skills training opportunities in technology fields. In addition, there are private sector efforts to support startups, including support from large banks such as TBC Bank and Bank of Georgia, new venture capital (VC) funds and angel investor networks, and, most importantly, community and nonprofit organizations such as Startup Büro or Impact Hub Tbilisi that are advocating for this cause. Additionally, there are a growing number of incubator and accelerator programs for early-stage startups, such as the 500 Georgia program. All these are explained in more detail in the following subsections.

Although several successful startups have emerged in Georgia, including a first international exit from Pulsar, an AI-based automotive software startup, the overall maturity of local startups is still low, and the ecosystem is still in the early stage of development. Startup Genome describes four phases in the development of a startup ecosystem, from activation to globalization and then to attraction and integration. Each phase has its own characteristics, challenges, and goals. As the collective startup experience grows and available resources increase, an ecosystem progresses through these phases (Startup Genome 2019). According to this classification, Georgia is currently in the first phase (activation) with limited startup know-how, scarce funding, and a small number of startups (Startup Genome 2020).

StartupBlink (2022) ranked Georgia 73rd out of 100 countries in its Global Startup Ecosystem Index. The ranking is based on the quantity and quality of startups in the country and the overall business environment. Among the cited drawbacks of Georgia's ecosystem are a lack of experienced entrepreneurs and limited private investment capital, as well as a small consumer market.[1]

Digital Infrastructure

In Georgia, access to digital infrastructure is increasing. The internet, with the mobile phone, has gradually replaced the fixed-line telephone as the primary form of communication. More than 80% of households have a fixed broadband connection,

---

[1] Compared with the neighboring countries, the most advanced startup ecosystem is found in the Russian Federation (17th), followed by Ukraine (34th), Türkiye (44th), and Armenia (65th). The only country behind Georgia (80th place) is Azerbaijan (89th place).

and more than 90% of companies with hired staff have access to the internet at work (GEOSTAT 2020). The country adopted the National Broadband Strategy in 2020, and efforts are under way to ensure high-quality 5G services. In addition to internet infrastructure, Georgia has actively worked to promote innovation and technological development by setting up technology parks (tech parks), fabrication laboratories (fablabs), and innovation centers with support from international donors.

Despite the relatively high level of digital uptake in Georgia compared with neighboring countries and other countries with the same income levels, there remains noteworthy digital access divide based on urban–rural and socioeconomic differences (UNECE 2020). There is also a significant gap in digital skills among the population, with lower skills in peripheral areas (USAID Georgia 2017). Along with household users, digitalization is not fully deployed by businesses, especially small and medium-sized enterprises (SMEs) outside Tbilisi.

For the country to harness the potential of the knowledge economy and support tech startups, infrastructure investments in ICT and digital inclusion programs are crucial. Development partners can and do play a vital role in this area. The European Union (EU) and the World Bank are making efforts through their respective programs, EU4Digital and Log-In Georgia. EU4Digital is an €11 million program to help Eastern Partnership states develop digital economies and societies by lowering roaming tariffs, developing high-speed broadband, expanding e-services, harmonizing digital frameworks from logistics to healthcare, building cybersecurity, developing skills, and creating jobs in digital industries.[2] Log-In Georgia is a World Bank project that provides broadband connectivity to over 1,000 communities and promotes digital literacy and inclusion.

Government Policies

General Business Climate

The government plays an important role in creating a suitable environment for entrepreneurship and startups. Favorable regulation, business licensing, and tax policies are fundamental pillars of a favorable business environment. Georgia experienced a turbulent economic transformation after regaining independence from the Soviet Union in 1991. The economy has been strengthened by economic reforms in recent decades that have strengthened the rule of law, improved governance, and increased foreign investment.

---

[2] The Eastern Partnership is an initiative of the EU, its member states, and Armenia, Azerbaijan, Belarus, Georgia, the Republic of Moldova, and Ukraine.

Georgia is the least corrupt country in the Black Sea region, according to the rankings of Transparency International (2020), outperforming EU countries. Georgia ranks seventh among 190 countries in the 2020 Ease of Doing Business Index (World Bank 2020a). The 2021 Index of Economic Freedom ranks Georgia 12th in the world and 7th in Europe. With an overall score above the regional and global average, the country outperforms its peers in both trade and business freedom (Heritage Foundation 2021). The overall business climate in Georgia is attractive to entrepreneurs, as business registration can be completed in less than 30 minutes, and startup founders noted the ease of streamlined tax procedures that can be completed through digitized platforms provided by the government's Revenue Service Agency. Senior managers in Georgia spend significantly less time on regulatory compliance than in other European and Central Asian or upper middle-income countries (World Bank 2020a, as above). In addition, managers of Georgian companies have to meet with tax officials only half as often as in other countries (World Bank 2019). The low level of corruption and minimal incidents of bribery are also reasons for the hassle-free working environment for businesses.

While it is easy to start a business in Georgia, the performance of local businesses in creating and adopting innovations is lagging. Georgia has a low score in resolving insolvencies, which can be a critical aspect for risk-taking and innovation (World Bank 2020a). The Global Competitiveness Index ranks Georgia 74th out of 141 countries, behind most in Europe and neighboring countries in the Caucasus (WEF 2019). According to the Global Competitiveness Index, weaknesses that may currently hinder startups include innovation capability (ranked 91), a lack of entrepreneurial culture (93), low growth of innovative companies (108), and limited availability of venture capital (119). Overall, political instability and access to finance remain pressing obstacles for businesses in Georgia, far more so than in European and Central Asian countries and in upper middle-income countries, according to the World Bank's Enterprise Survey (World Bank 2019).

Policies and Programs for Startups and Innovation

In 2014, the government established Georgia's Innovation and Technology Agency (GITA), under the Ministry of Economy and Sustainable Development. This action indicates that advancing the technology ecosystem is a government priority. This was followed by the adoption of the Law on Innovation in 2016 and the efforts of the National Intellectual Property Center of Georgia – Sakpatenti to promote intellectual property protection and awareness among innovative entrepreneurs.

Government support for the tech startup ecosystem has primarily focused on providing digital training, technology parks and innovation centers, and grants to early-stage startups. GITA treats all sectors equally including agritech, cleantech, edtech, and healthtech. There are some specific initiatives such as GITA's collaboration with the United States Agency for International Development (USAID) on agri-bio-foodtech acceleration.

Many of the startups interviewed indicated that there are no specific tax exemptions or incentives for startups. Startups are not registered as a different legal entity than other small, medium-sized, or large enterprises. In fact, all registered startups are considered limited liability companies and must meet the standard tax requirements. Most taxes relevant to businesses are 20% personal income tax, 4% pension contribution, 15% corporate (profit) tax, and 18% value-added tax (VAT). General rates on imported goods are 0%, 5%, and 12% depending on the type of project. Import tax is relevant for hardware-based technology startups that depend on component and material imports from foreign manufacturers, such as the People's Republic of China (PRC) and other countries. Any imported product worth more than $90 (GEL300) is subject to import tax. Ramaz Javakhishvili, cofounder of Farco, an agritech startup that manufactures remote greenhouse control systems, suggested that removing or increasing the value cap on prototype components would benefit early-stage hardware-based startups. There are several public or private petitions to raise the taxable product value from GEL300 to GEL700, but the government has not yet made any changes.

> "When you are building hardware, you need multiple components and might need to import different options, until you find the right match and combination of materials for your purposes. At these preliminary stages, before there is a working prototype or a proof of concept, most of the founders rely on their personal money, and any savings or incentives could help us move faster."
>
> *(Ramaz Javakhishvili, cofounder of Farco)*

Most companies begin paying VAT (18%) when their cumulative sales (over one or more years) reach about $30,000 (GEL100,000). In recent years, there have been discussions about raising this cap for tech companies, but no legislation has yet been submitted to Parliament.

In 2010, Georgia introduced a virtual economic zone for companies developing information technology (IT) services in the country. These companies do not pay VAT or taxes on their profits. Over the course of 10 years, more than 1,000 companies have registered for virtual economic zone status (Business Media Georgia 2021). The virtual economic zone is not actively promoted by the government, and it is hardly known in the technology community. None of the startups interviewed knew about the tax benefits of the virtual economic zone.

In 2020, the government introduced the international company status, which grants reduced tax rates to eligible companies in the IT sector that serve international customers (at least 90% of revenues come from outside Georgia) (Government of Georgia 2020). The broad list of eligible activities includes software development, computer programming, creation and provision of digital services, and other activities (hardware production is not included). To qualify for international company status, the company must have been providing relevant services in Georgia for more than 2 years, either itself or through a subsidiary of an international company. Businesses with international company status pay 5% corporate income tax (instead of 15%), their employees pay 5% income tax (instead of 20%), there is no withholding tax on dividends (instead of 20%), and the business is exempt from property tax (other than land).[3] There are no restrictions or limits on the volume of business activity or duration for the incentives.

International company status was introduced to encourage foreign direct investment in the technology sector and to create a supportive environment for outsourcing companies that hire local talent while serving global markets. As a result, there is already growing interest from international companies to expand to Georgia or move their operations there altogether. Examples include IT outsourcing companies EPAM Systems, Inc., and Exadel, Inc., which have entered the market and become the largest employers in the country's technology sector, employing hundreds of people. While these tax incentives may be attractive to international companies, they do not serve local IT companies or tech startups that are in still in the product development phase and do not (yet) serve international customers. In addition, Rakuten Group, Inc., which uses international company status, is in the process of opening an office in Tbilisi to develop mobile applications for its popular messaging product, Viber (Agenda.GE 2022). Irakli Kashibadze, cofounder of GoandGrow, said that "startups need more support as they do not go through standard processes, but are in pilot mode with constant changes. This is not a business. Startups become businesses only when they find product-market fit; before that, it's more like "research-mode."

> "For tech startups most of the costs are associated with salaries especially at early stages when you are developing a product. Financial resources at that time are typically scarce. Having decreased personal income tax alone could help startups to reinvest, hire additional staff, and grow faster."
>
> *(Vato Veliashvili, CEO of Lingwing)*

---

[3] Property tax (other than land) exempt if the property is used only for activities allowed under the status (instead of the regular percentage, which is up to 1% depending on the type of property, and the exemption does not include property tax on land).

Finance

Access to adequate funding is essential for a proactive entrepreneurial ecosystem. Globally, tech startups often cite limited access to capital as one of their biggest challenges, and Georgia is no exception. This report goes beneath the tip of the iceberg to identify specific funding opportunities at different stages of the startup life cycle. The four sectors of interest (agritech, cleantech, edtech, and healthtech) are discussed in detail.

Government Programs

The government is a main provider of capital to early-stage tech startups. GITA offers startups grants of up to GEL650,000. The grants are distributed through the government's budget, as well as the World Bank's Georgia National Innovation Ecosystem (GENIE) program, which was launched in 2016 and runs through 2023 with a total cost of $23.4 million. GENIE is designed to strengthen and develop the innovation ecosystem through the provision of innovation infrastructure and services, ecosystem support, and funding. Table 1 (page 10) illustrates the type and amount of funding provided by GITA to local startups since 2015. The maximum level of grant and program requirements has changed over the years to adapt to the needs of the local ecosystem and to grantee feedback. In addition to startup support, GITA's small grants programs have funded initiatives such as tech and entrepreneurship events and conferences in Georgia or travel support for Georgian tech talent or startups to attend international conferences, trade shows, etc. over the years (2015–2019). Startup matching grants require the grantee to provide 10% cofinancing of the total project amount. The innovation matching grants are designed to attract private investment, as grants are matched one on one with the amount secured by the private investment (up to GEL650,000). All grant proposals are completed based on templates provided by GITA, and narrative proposals and budget allocations must serve a specific purpose for startup growth and expansion. GITA grantees must follow financial reporting procedures and approve any budget changes in advance.

Table 1: Funding Programs by Georgia's Innovation and Technology Agency, 2015–2022

Grant Programs	Number of Funded Projects/Startups over the Years								
	2015	2016	2017	2018	2019	2020	2021	2022	Total
Small grants program (up to GEL5,000)	47	82	62	98	124				413
Prototyping grants program (up to GEL15,000)						27	31	16	74
Pilot program for regional development (up to GEL30,000 or GEL100,000 grants for business ideas and startups in specific regions, outside Tbilisi)								48	48
Startup matching grants (up to GEL100,000)				17	39	39	40		135
Startup matching grants (up to GEL150,000)								20	20
Innovation matching grants (up to GEL650,000)					4	10	10		24
Total Number of Projects/Startups Funded									**714**

Source: Data provided by Georgia's Innovation and Technology Agency.

By mid-2021, more than 280 startups had received GITA grants totaling GEL21.9 million. Avtandil Kasradze, chairman of GITA, noted that the quantity and quality of Georgian startups has increased over the years, both in terms of applicants and successful grantees.[4]

Startups interested in receiving funding from GITA complete an online application and, if successful in the first stage, are invited to present their idea to a panel of judges. For the startup matching grants, shortlisted startups go through several training sessions before presenting to an international panel in English. The pitching process and award ceremony are streamed live to the public through YouTube and Facebook. The startups are assessed based on six key criteria: (i) team competence, (ii) market size/potential, (iii) value proposition, (iv) business model, (v) market entry strategy, and (vi) competitive advantage.

GITA's startup matching grants are available to "initiative groups" (i.e., nonestablished entities or groups of individuals or budding entrepreneurs) or registered limited liability companies that have been in operation for less than 2 years and have not yet generated annual revenues in excess of GEL500,000. Additionally, the duration of the proposed activities should not exceed 9 months.

Agritech, cleantech, edtech, and healthtech startups account for about 20% of GITA's successful proposals. The distribution of these startups is shown in Table 2 (page 11). Due to the small size of the data, no trends (e.g., distribution by sector) can be detected over time. To date, only healthtech startups, among the four sectors, have received larger amounts of startup matching grants and innovation matching grants.

---

[4]   Interview with the authors.

Table 2: Startups Funded by GITA's Grant Programs, 2015–2021

Grant Program	Total Startups Funded	Cleantech	Edtech	Healthtech
Prototype grants (max. GEL15,000)	156	6 (3.8%)	7 (4.5%)	10 (6.4%)
Startup matching grants (max. GEL100,000)	111	5 (4.5%)	4 (3.6%)	5 (4.5%)
Innovation matching grants (max. GEL650,000)	15	0	0	3 (20%)
Total Funded	**282**	**11**	**11**	**18**

GITA = Georgia's Innovation and Technology Agency, max. = maximum.
Note: Figures in parentheses represent the share of that sector in total grants for each program.
Source: ADB estimates using data provided to the authors by GITA in 2021.

The GITA grant is described by both startups and ecosystem players as a stimulator for the creation of new tech startups or the development of those that move beyond the prototype phase. The program is aimed at first-time entrepreneurs, and applicants do not have to be official legal entities. The grants help entrepreneurs avoid risks (as they are not loans or equity) while providing cash flow to attract tech talent or pay for marketing costs. In addition to financial support, GITA provides startups with mentoring, training, access to Silicon Valley experts and a panel of judges, and networking with other startups in the local ecosystem. Some of the best-performing GITA-funded startups are given the opportunity to showcase themselves to potential partners and investors by taking business trips to the United States (US) or attending local and international conferences.

In addition to the positive aspects of GITA programs, the startups and stakeholders interviewed also highlighted the drawbacks. Some argue that GITA's grants are not flexible enough to adapt to the nature of startups, which are subject to constant change. The proposal submitted for the grant program may need to be modified after implementation begins. Changes to the budget and priorities are possible but require approval by the program. Unexpended budget items cannot be reallocated to other activities without approval. Grant recipients may overspend on a budget item by 15% (with the exception of salaries), but additional changes require written justification and may be rejected by GITA. In extreme cases, GITA may terminate the grant if the startup cannot meet its milestones. In this case, the grantee may be required to return the grant amount, possibly including partial or full repayment of funds already spent.

With respect to the four sectors which are the focus of this report, GITA's prototyping and startup matching grants may not provide sufficient funding for cleantech, healthtech, and agritech startups to cover research and development (R&D) and other early-stage costs. However, once such startups mature, they can apply for innovation matching grants, which can be up to GEL650,000, with an equal amount of coinvestment from the private sector.

While GITA's grants have inspired many first-time entrepreneurs to establish startups, some ecosystem players note that founders view these grants as ends in themselves rather than as means to an end. Their focus on obtaining grants diverts their attention from validating the product and business model in the marketplace with consumers (and not just with the grant competition judges). The judges may be less critical than investors seeking a return on investment. Startups with a narrow grant-winning focus often struggle to develop and gain traction with consumers and investors when the grant money runs out.

> "We, as a government, took a leap of faith in Georgia's technology ecosystem and decided to fund technology startups as it was a nascent field, and there was skepticism from the private sector. After 2026, we aim to stop direct financing and will use the period between now and then to encourage more private sector investment."
>
> *(Avtandil Kasradze, chairman of GITA)*

While GITA is the main government institution providing grants, the table in Appendix 3 shows other funding opportunities for startups through the Enterprise Georgia agency and Startup Georgia program. None of the 23 startups interviewed considered or applied for government funding programs other than GITA. Despite the drawbacks mentioned previously, GITA grants are popular because they are tailored to technology startups and provide a grant (i.e., not an equity stake). Some grants require the startup to provide or secure a matching investment which can be small (10%) or larger (50%) depending on the program.[5]

In summary, government grant programs enable early-stage or first-time entrepreneurs to get started with their business ideas. From the interviews, it appears that this has helped make a career as a startup founder attractive to young talent, and it has created momentum for early-stage startups. GITA estimates that of the more than 280 startups funded through the grant programs (GEL20 million), these startups have received additional investment of $95 million from private investors, both domestic and foreign.[6]

---

[5] In addition, the European Bank for Reconstruction and Development (EBRD) initiated the Star Venture Program in 2022 that provides an 18-month program of training, guidance, and networking. The program also offers cost-recovery grants to pay for consulting services and travel to international conferences and competitions. The program covers 30 countries, and two Georgian startups were accepted in late 2022. EBRD Star Venture Programme. Start-ups.

[6] Information provided to authors by a GITA representative.

Loans

Bank loans are not a common source of capital for technology startups. Banks view startups as risky and uncertain ventures. It is difficult for startups to service loans on a regular basis (i.e., monthly or quarterly) because they have little or no revenue in the early stages. Collateral is hard to provide given the intangibility of technology products.

However, Georgia's banking and microcredit sector has special loan programs tailored to small businesses and startups. For example, TBC Bank launched Startuperi in 2017 to support SMEs. By 2021, some 55,000 SMEs had been registered for the program's various activities, which include training, business networking meetings, and workshops, in addition to loans and leases. The bank provides startup loans of up to GEL15,000 without collateral or cofinancing and up to GEL100,000 for innovative startups with a maturity of up to 7 years. The program had 493 active loans totaling GEL196.9 million at the end of 2021 (TBC 2021). The company positions itself as a supporter of young entrepreneurs and creativity.

It is important to note that not all of them are technology-based, as TBC Bank considers any type of new business to be a startup, whether or not it uses digital or other innovative technology. This approach is generally followed by other financial institutions in the country (e.g., Bank of Georgia, Credo, Crystal). They treat startups the same as other SMEs and have no specific programs for enterprises developing software, hardware, or other tech solutions. The Bank of Georgia, in partnership with the European Bank for Reconstruction and Development (EBRD), has introduced a similar program, Female Start Upper program, but it is not focused on technology. The program offers women founders loans ranging from GEL10,000 to GEL100,000 with a maturity up to 5 years. No cofinancing or coinvestment by the founder is required.

One of the programs worth noting is InnovFin, an initiative of the European Investment Bank and Horizon 2020, a research and innovation program of the European Commission. InnovFin supports projects that are riskier and more difficult to assess than traditional investments and therefore often have difficulty accessing funding. Funding is provided to support research and innovation by small tech startups as well as larger companies, large research facilities, and circular economy companies. In Georgia, the program is implemented by ProCredit Bank, which provides investment and working capital loans. A credit guarantee is provided, which allows a company to provide 50% less collateral than they normally would. Loan amounts vary from €25,000 to €7.5 million.

In addition, the EBRD offers loans through the Green Economy Financing Facility, which is provided through ProCredit Bank, TBC Bank, and Basis Bank. The funds are provided to SMEs and large companies for investments in energy-efficient, renewable energy, and green initiatives. The Green Economy Financing Facility funding allows companies to purchase technology from Technology Selector's green technology platform,[7] or implement multicomponent green projects and receive a free technical assessment and funding. The funding program supports investments in energy-efficient machinery, energy-efficiency improvements of existing buildings, investments to save at least 20% water or sustainable land management, and investments in renewable energy technologies. Loans of up to $300,000 are available for small and well-defined projects, and up to $1 million or $5 million for large-scale energy efficiency and renewable energy projects.

Another line of credit is provided to domestic banks by EU4Business, an EU initiative. The loans from the banks will be used to finance fixed assets for enterprises with fewer than 250 employees. A grant of 15% of the loan amount is also provided (EU4Business 2020). About €16 million was triggered in the form of structured funds and more than €10 million in the form of grants.

In the agriculture sector, Enterprise Georgia partners with banks in providing working capital and financing fixed asset investments as part of the preferential agro credit program to improve primary agricultural production, processing, storage, and sales. Loan amounts can range from GEL7,000 to GEL15 million. The government's Rural Development Agency provides a form of cofinancing by shouldering interest payments for up to 12.5 years at an annual interest rate of 8% to 18%.

The above finance programs do not specifically target startups in the agritech, cleantech, edtech, and healthtech sectors, but startups in these sectors can apply and gain access. Access is more likely at the growth stage when there is already a product or service on the market. From interviews, it appears that most startups have little knowledge or understanding of the funding options available from financial institutions.

Financing is also important to startups' customers. For example, if a cleantech startup develops an environmentally friendly business-to-business (B2B) solution, its customers may need access to credit to purchase the technology from the startup.

---

[7] A global shopping-style platform that connects vendors of the green technologies with forward-thinking businesses and homeowners. See Green Technology Selector.

In summary, there are several loan programs that startups are eligible for, but according to the interviews, this financing model is not preferred by startups, especially in the early stages when the risks are high, there is not yet a product or even a prototype, and the entrepreneurs are still running their startup as a side business. Even though many financial institutions give small businesses a grace period of 1 year, entrepreneurs are not sure if they would be generating revenue even after a year, especially if they have to do technical product development and testing first. Vato Veliashvili, CEO of Lingwing, a language learning tool, said that his startup has never considered a loan. "If we needed additional capital to expand to a new country, a loan would be the least favorable option," he said.

> "Banks are typically more oriented on taking lower risks and expect stable payments from the debtor, which can't be guaranteed with startups."
> (Irakli Kashibadze, founder of GoandGrow)

Additionally, the ratio of household debt to gross domestic product (GDP) is high in Georgia.[8] People who want to start their own business may already have financial obligations to banks (e.g., mortgages, consumer loans). Due to this local characteristic, entrepreneurs who already have loan obligations may refrain from taking on new commitments by relying on personal income or family property to provide collateral for a startup loan. Or the founder may not have additional property to put up as collateral.

In summary, Georgia's early-stage startups currently have more flexible and less onerous opportunities provided by grants, which do not require repayment or interest charges. This has reduced their interest in taking out bank loans.

Venture Capital and Angel Investing

The venture capital market in Georgia is at an early stage of development. Recently, several groups have emerged to promote venture capital and develop a network of angel investors.

Georgia's Law on Promotion and Guarantees of Investment Activity was enacted in 2006 (Legislative Herald of Georgia 2006). This law establishes the legal basis for and protection of foreign and local investments in Georgia. In 2020, the government passed the Law on Investment of Funds (Legislative Herald of Georgia 2020). The aim of this law is to develop the market for investment funds, ensure competition in the market, and protect the interests of investors. It governs venture capital. These laws provide the regulatory framework for globally integrated portfolio investments, i.e., capital markets that can provide Georgian businesses

---

[8]   National Bank of Georgia. Statistics Data.

with diversified sources of capital from home or abroad. This will promote Georgia's economic growth in two ways: it will make it easier for Georgian investors to trade in foreign markets, and it will give Georgian businesses access to international capital to expand their businesses.

Investment companies and individual investors in and outside Georgia are showing increasing interest in technology startups. Some of these examples are listed below (Appendix 4 has more detailed information). For example, one of the largest investment funds in the country, Georgia Capital, provided $3.2 million to Redberry Startup Studio to offer incubator programs and equity investments for tech startups (CBW 2019).

In addition, GITA signed a memorandum with TECH Friends of Georgia, an investment fund that connects US investors with Georgia startups. GITA will help identify local startups with global potential that can receive connections to California-based startups and up to $500,000 in equity funding. The initiative is still in its early stages, and no deals have been made yet. Currently in the development stage, Catapult Ventures, a California-based company that invests in technology ventures, is launching a fund to invest in innovative startups in Georgia. Called Catapult Georgia I, LP, the fund aims to raise $50 million. It will work with the US Market Access Center and Startup Grind Tbilisi to provide both capital and mentorship to approximately 50 Georgian startups over the next decade (Investor.ge 2021a). The fund is currently in the fundraising phase and has not yet made any investments.

In the academic sector, the Business and Technology University has recently established a Global Startup Foundation with Georgian–Israeli angel investors who occasionally interact with Georgian startups through pitching events. There is no data on how many actual investments or partnerships have come from this.

Another new initiative is Axel, a network of angel investors founded by Startup Büro and Kedari Ventures, which brings together investors from Georgia and the European countries. For paying members who are experienced or wealthy investors, Axel organizes closed monthly meetings where selected startups pitch, share information about their ongoing investment round, and respond to questions from participants. The network has heard pitches from 58 startups and, as of October 2022, had invested in seven of them, including Theneo, a Software-as-a-Service (SaaS) solution that helps developers create efficient technical documentation.[9] The investment was made through a special purpose vehicle (SPV).

[9] Theneo was founded by software engineers who acquired their education and work experience in the US. The startup obtained a grant from GITA for GEL100,000 and up to $1 million in total funding. It has also been accepted to Y Combinator, a renowned accelerator program that provides equity funding and training.

SPVs typically pool the money of a group of investors to invest in a single company. The main difference between an SPV and a fund is that an SPV makes a single investment in only one company, while a fund invests in multiple companies. In Georgia, SPVs do not have a specific or special legal form. Axel's SPVs (one for each investment) are established as standard limited liability companies. According to the Law on Investment of Funds (Legislative Herald of Georgia 2020), a fund may be established as a joint stock company. A closed-end registered investment company may also be registered as a limited liability company or a limited partnership under the Law on Entrepreneurs. Under this law, a registered investment fund may not have more than 20 retail investors, while an authorized investment fund may have more than 20.

Another SPV that invested in Theneo was established by Cartooli, an initiative led by a Georgian-American duo that helps first-time investors or experienced angels invest in Georgian startups. Cartooli handles deal execution and due diligence and has a more open structure than Axel (no membership fees, any interested party can obtain information and join the SPV). Individuals can invest from as little as $1,000, depending on the terms of each startup. In the case of Cartooli, the process is streamlined through Assure, a software platform, and no legal entities are established in Georgia. Assure is a software platform for creating and managing SPVs and investments.

Wealth on Wings is another initiative supported locally by the World Bank to help women in technology and business learn about angel investing and become investors. It offers training on investing, insights into local startups, and tips on conducting due diligence.

Other entities supporting private investment in startups include Georgian Venture Capital Association (GVCA) and the Angel Investor Club Georgia—both of which are in their early stages. Founded in 2017, GVCA works with its up to 10 members and partners to develop the venture capital and private equity industry to stimulate innovation and growth. GVCA provides a collective voice to various government agencies, regulatory bodies, and other stakeholders.[10] The Angel Investor Club Georgia collectively invests between $30,000 and $200,000 in a startup, from the idea stage through to Series A funding rounds. Depending on the stage of the startup, angels participate in equity funding or provide either revenue-based funding or convertible debt. There is no public data on how many deals they have already closed.[11]

---

[10] Georgian Venture Capital Association.
[11] Angel Investor Club Georgia.

Currently, none of the initiatives or institutions listed have a specific focus on agritech, edtech, cleantech, and healthtech, but startups in all four areas may pursue funding options with these stakeholders. None of the startups interviewed have approached a domestic investment fund or angel investor. Investments by existing venture capital firms in the clean energy, agriculture, or healthcare sectors tend to go to large businesses in those sectors, rather than startups. However, large venture capital firms consider supporting education and the environment as part of their corporate social responsibility—a characteristic that startups seeking funds could use to their advantage. This development could lead to impact investing, which is not yet practiced in Georgia.

Several independent angels and investment companies have invested in early-stage startups in Georgia. Pulsar had its first international exit when it was purchased by US-based SpinCar, now known as Impel. Some of the angel investors saw the benefit of reaping their investments and earning higher returns. However, the venture capital scene is still very young, and its activities and transaction flows are limited. All of the VC funds and angel networks mentioned above are nascent and have yet to become properly institutionalized. Interactions are largely based on personal contacts, and most startups do not know how to approach VCs or angels. Given the premature state, information about how to secure or provide venture and angel investment is still limited on both sides. The founders and teams of startups lack knowledge about investments and financial literacy.

Stakeholders mention that the so-called investment readiness among local startups is low, as most of them are at an early stage and it is not clear whether they are ready and equipped to receive investment and take the next steps. At the same time, traditional investors are not fully aware of the characteristics of tech startups and expect quick investment returns, higher equity, and low risk.

Many of the startups indicated that what is lacking in Georgia is not access to funding, but access to "smart money." This means meaning that an investor, whether VC or an individual angel, has a solid understanding of the type of startups or the specific industry and is able to help a startup grow through mentoring and access to networks and markets. Additionally, there are currently no tax incentives for individual investors to fund tech startups. Hayk Asriyants, cofounder of Axel, said that in order to promote and develop angel investing, the country can follow best practices and introduce incentives.

> "For instance, Norway has introduced tax relief as an incentive for angel investors who make investments in early-stage startups."
>
> *(Hayk Asriyants, cofounder of Startup Büro and Axel)*

Most of the startups interviewed have not currently announced active fundraising rounds, nor are they proactively approaching investors. Large companies are investing in their subsidiaries or in other startups that have experience and social capital in the ecosystem. BioChimPharm, for example, is a natural phage producer established by its parent company (which itself was originally a public research center that was privatized as a company). It is currently establishing subcompanies to develop innovative products. In healthtech, the main startups are focused on telemedicine—RedMed and Ekimo— which were founded by established large corporations in Georgia, TBC Insurance and Georgian Healthcare Group, respectively. SpaceFarms was also cofounded by the Adjara Group. EduPay, a payment system for educational institutions, secured its initial capital through personal connections from an individual investor, and Agronavti, a platform that connects local farmers with knowledge and markets, received small equity funding from the Bank of Georgia under the 500 Startups Accelerator program.

It is important to understand that Georgian startups are not limited to raising capital locally, but also have access to foreign VC funds or individual foreign investors. There are a handful of such cases, though none in the four startup sectors covered in this report. In the interviews, cleantech startups seemed most interested in approaching international investors, especially in Europe and the US. However, they indicated that they do not have sufficient contacts or networks to approach investors and conduct negotiations. In addition, many foreign investment funds are not particularly interested in or focused on Georgian startups. Since the startup scene as a whole is still young and there are only a few successful examples, foreign VC firms and investors lack confidence in the quality and reliability of Georgian startups. Some local startups have found a way around this challenge by establishing a legal entity in the US (C Corporation) or a virtual enterprise in Estonia, i.e., in the EU, under the country's e-resident program. However, this practice, is used by a very few companies in Georgia, and most startup teams lack information and know-how about these procedures.

Prize Money and Donor Grants

In Georgia, participating in hackathons and grant competitions is a common way for startups to gain access to initial small amounts of funds with which to begin building a prototype.

International donors that are operating in Georgia, such as the United Nations Development Programme (UNDP), the United States Agency for International Development (USAID), the EBRD, the European Fund for Southeast Europe (EFSE), the EU, and others are increasingly supporting and organizing competitions and training programs that help young Georgians establish startups that serve social and environmental goals. Given the impact startups could have in our four targeted sectors, the potential for funding from international donors is promising.

For example, Zrda is a USAID program that supports agricultural innovation by funding technology initiatives such as the app Agronavti. Startup Büro organizes the annual Future Agro Challenge for agri-food startups. The initiative is supported and funded by public–private partners such as GITA, USAID, and Liberty Bank.

Large banks in Georgia often organize competitions, such as Bank of Georgia's fintech hackathons and TBC Bank's B2B Solutions Challenge. Universities hold business idea competitions and hackathons for students. In 2021, for example, Ilia State University organized a hackathon to promote the creation of tools or games for digital education. The hackathon was associated with DigiEduHack, a Europe-wide initiative supported by the EU and other institutions. International groups such as Startup Wise Guys, SeedStars, and TechStars have also organized hackathons and pitching competitions in the country, mostly as one-off events. In addition, prize money in the form of grants or equity investments is provided by some incubators and accelerators, including the Business and Technology University accelerator and 500 Startups Georgia.

Social entrepreneurship is also gaining attention as more development organizations and companies offer support. The Europe Fund has a special program to support the establishment of social enterprises. The Bank of Georgia's Tree of Life program offers grants up to GEL50,000 to start a social enterprise. However, the grants are mostly given to traditional businesses or to minority or rural communities that lack the technological skills to create startups. The Impact Hub Tbilisi Social Impact Award, a program that is part of a global movement, offers incubation and pitching competitions for early-stage social enterprises and is supported by several private and nonprofit institutions in Georgia. Although some applicants have used technology for social good, most ideas are based on traditional business models. Social entrepreneurship based on technological solutions need more support. This could further encourage the emergence of startups in agritech, cleantech, edtech, and healthtech.

Georgia relies heavily on international donors to fund social initiatives, with grants mostly directed to nonprofit organizations and funding specific activities and beneficiaries (e.g., skills development, women's empowerment, traditional SMEs, etc.). However, some startups in the edtech and agritech sectors (e.g., Nebula, Agronavti) have been able to find an overlap between their business goals and the objectives of these grant programs and thus secure funding. However, such cases are the exception rather than the rule. Donors usually refrain from investing equity in startups because it may be against their guidelines or require more resources than they have. In addition, direct social impact is often difficult to measure in technology startups, especially in a short time frame as required by the grant program. The risk and novelty of startups also contribute to international donors' reluctance to fund startups directly.

Crowdfunding and Peer-to-Peer Lending

Peer-to-peer lending and crowdfunding are still very new to Georgia's entrepreneurial scene. Orbeliani, a local nonprofit organization, offers social and entrepreneurial initiatives the means to raise money through its online platform. Orbeliani not only provides a digital platform where all amounts donated by individuals are visible, but also matches the funds and becomes an investor itself. Fundraiser.ge is another new crowdfunding platform.

Despite some examples and transactions in recent years, these methods are not yet widespread, scalable, or sustainable. Most crowdfunding projects are for social community initiatives rather than for-profit tech startups. None of the founders interviewed had used crowdfunding before, and many lack even an understanding of the technical and legal details involved, especially when it involves equity crowdfunding. International crowdfunding platforms such as Kickstarter, Indiegogo, or GoFundMe do not allow account registration from Georgia. Georgia lacks a clear tax and legal framework to determine what crowdfunding is and how intermediary online platforms or organizations managing peer-to-peer lending and crowdfunding should be treated, although some legislative changes are in the works. Furthermore, stakeholders attribute the low adoption of such practices to a lack of trust, awareness, and interest in them. In Georgia, most crowdfunding processes are empathy-driven, and there is not much interest in equity investment in private businesses. Even when crowdfunding is used, the funds generated are too small to develop prototypes, especially for resource- and innovation-intensive initiatives such as cleantech.

There is a clear lack of legal framework and awareness of crowdfunding and peer-to-peer lending in Georgia, and it can be difficult to integrate and use international platforms locally.

Personal Savings, Friends, and Family

Bootstrapping—using one's own financial (and human) resources to develop a minimum viable product—is very rare among the startups interviewed (BioDiesel and SchoolBook are exceptions). The savings habit is not very strong in Georgia, as 84% of people do not typically set aside money from their salary each month. Low income discourages 70% of the population from saving (ACT Research 2011). As a result, it is not common to ask family and friends for money.

Nevertheless, employees in the technology sector earn high salaries compared with the national average. In addition, people who work in outsourcing receive a competitive international salary that allows them to save money. Founders in Georgia may not invest a large portion of their personal funds in startups, but they pay for startup costs from the salary they earn at their current jobs. While this approach sounds convenient, it hinders the founder's ability to fully commit to the startup as they are simultaneously working a regular job. GITA grants, for example, are not generous enough to invest in software and customer development while paying the founder's salary.

Market Characteristics

Overall Review

Startups primarily focus on developing innovative solutions that fill a gap in an existing market or create a new market. Georgia is often described as a small consumer market due to its population (3.7 million people) and GDP per capita of around $4,000.[12] For technology startups, small local customer segments further filtered by limited digital adoption levels and weak purchasing power lead to a small potential market. StartupBlink, the global startup ecosystem mapping and research center, places Georgia in the bottom 30 of 100 countries based on ecosystem quantity, startup quality, and business environment. Among other limitations, StartupBlink considers the small market size as a challenge for local startups (StartupBlink 2022).

However, globalization and the emergence of digital systems that span national borders provide opportunities for startups to expand their market. The world is open for business, and startups are not limited to their domestic market. Most successful startups were designed with a scalable business model in mind. This opens new opportunities for startups from small countries like Georgia. Stakeholders mention that Georgia could be a convenient launching ground for both domestic and international startup founders looking to serve global markets. The general business climate is comfortable. There are significant tax benefits for technology companies serving markets outside Georgia, and tech labor is more affordable than in Europe. Georgia's strategic location at the crossroads of Europe, Asia, and the Middle East is also an important opportunity to exploit. In this regard, some of the local startups (mainly in fintech) have already expanded to Central Asia (e.g., Uzbekistan) and Eastern Europe (e.g., Ukraine, Estonia). Lingwing is simultaneously operating in Georgia, Armenia, and Bangladesh, with plans to expand to the US and the United Kingdom. BioChimPharm already sells in eight countries of the Commonwealth of Independent States, including Armenia, Azerbaijan, Kazakhstan, Moldova, and the Russian Federation.

---

[12] World Bank. World Development Indicators. GDP per capita (current US$) – Georgia.

Georgia joined a number of free trade agreements (FTAs), including the Deep and Comprehensive Free Trade Agreement with the EU in 2014, which opened unprecedented access to markets and led to reforms in areas such as standardization, accreditation, technical regulations, and dispute settlement. In 2018, a bilateral FTA was signed with the People's Republic of China (PRC). Georgia achieved a trade intensity of 122% of GDP in 2018, well above neighboring Türkiye (60%) and the Russian Federation (52%) (UNECE 2020). While FTAs are becoming more common for Georgia, they still tend to focus on traditional industries.

According to the interviews, global expansion is not an integral part of the strategy of Georgian startups in the four sectors studied. The reasons for this are a general lack of product maturity—products based on local aspects of the Georgian market need to be heavily modified to capture the characteristics of other markets (e.g., language, institutional differences in education and healthcare systems)—and a lack of confidence, know-how, and international connections among founders.

Understanding the dynamics of foreign markets is critical. Founders planning to expand outside Georgia may have a general idea of where the potential demand might be, but may lack in-depth understanding of the market, so they are unable to develop an appropriate strategy for market penetration.

Startups thinking about scaling up tend to have one of two geographic orientations: (i) toward countries with similar socioeconomic contexts, such as nearby former Soviet Union states like Armenia, Uzbekistan, Kazakhstan, and the Baltic states; or (ii) toward the US.

Expanding the operations of a startup that produces hardware or other tangible products requires more resources than digital startups. This is especially critical for agritech and cleantech startups (e.g., SpaceFarms, Enovus, BioDiesel).

> There is also a general feeling that "Made in Georgia" products do not represent quality or trust among consumers and businesses in Europe and the US. To grow, we need to produce the product somewhere else, for example, partner with a commercial lab in the US that could do it.
> *(Murman Pataraia, cofounder and CEO of BioDiesel)*

Georgian startups have the opportunity to expand and integrate into neighboring or global markets, but they need support from the government as well as private investors, consulting firms, and the Georgian diaspora. Support can take the form of lowering barriers to entry and empowering local startups with market research, strategies for global expansion, and access to relevant professional networks and mentors.

There was a case where GITA organized a trip to Silicon Valley for selected technology startups and significantly impacted the growth of at least one participant. AI startup Pulsar recruited a US-based cofounder who helped the company identify an important gap in the automobile sales industry, based on which Pulsar developed new software. The startup was later acquired by Spincar, a major player in the US automobile industry. It was the first international exit of a Georgia-born startup (Investor.ge 2021b). GITA has also organized study visits to Israel, Italy, and Poland in collaboration with diplomatic and technology partners in those countries.

An interesting new player in the ecosystem is Globalize, a private company operating since March 2022. It promotes Georgian products and services in global markets and helps startups to enter new markets. Globalize initially brought together Georgian professionals in 12 countries[13] to share their knowledge and experience with startups and exporters. This brings together more than 6,000 Georgian startup supporters outside the country. Currently, the country associations and their Georgian diaspora provide startups with various services such as market research, legal services, local partner search, investor outreach, global marketing and branding, market entry strategies, etc. In addition, Globalize has partner communication agencies in more than 50 countries that can help startups with marketing and communication in new markets. Another important activity of Globalize is organizing conferences and workshops for startups in different countries, where they can make new contacts with representatives of the diaspora and present their startup to local investors. One conference is planned per quarter. Globalize cooperates with the private sector in Georgia (Bank of Georgia, Business and Technology University, Nexia TA) and the government (GITA) in the implementation of its activities. Moreover, Globalize funds its activities through annual membership fees for startups and exporters using its services.

> "Many interesting projects and startup ideas appear in the market; however, we have a lot of work to do in terms of developing a global vision so that ideas are properly integrated into international markets and startups are able to expand and adjust to new customer segments. There are many factors to consider, [such as a] lack of reliable partners and connections, legal issues and bureaucracy, lack of resources on the ground, language and cultural barriers, ethnocentrism, etc. Globalize was created to overcome these obstacles and promote Georgian business to enter global markets, which will combine many necessary resources in one space to achieve success on the mentioned path."
>
> *(Salome Kukava, CEO of Globalize)*

---

[13] The US, the United Kingdom, Israel, Kazakhstan, Uzbekistan, Switzerland, France, Germany, Spain, Poland, Italy, and the United Arab Emirates.

Agritech, cleantech, edtech, and healthtech are growing industries worldwide, and Georgia could secure a position in them if its startups are properly supported. Although there are not yet many startups in these four areas, Georgia's technology scene is growing and various Software-as-a-Service (SaaS), AI, and fintech solutions are becoming available. Georgian startups could leverage existing expertise and adapt it to market needs, for example by using AI in agriculture or fintech in education (e.g., to pay tuition). The following sections discuss the local market characteristics of the four industries and their readiness for tech startups.

Agritech

Agriculture has traditionally been considered one of the cornerstones of the Georgian economy. About 40% of the population lives in rural areas, and 39% of the country's total workforce is engaged in agriculture (GEOSTAT 2014). However, the share of commercial farms in agricultural production remains low, as most farmers practice subsistence farming, sometimes with a small surplus for sale, and nearly 94% of agricultural households own less than 2 hectares of land. Although a large part of the population is engaged in agriculture, it contributes only 8% to GDP.

The government supports the sector significantly through various programs and funding. Government programs are mainly social in nature and do not aim to increase economic efficiency. In 2013–2019, the government spent GEL1.5 billion on agricultural development. During the same period, agricultural production grew by 1.5% annually, which was one-third of the growth rate of the overall economy (Transparency International Georgia 2020). Agriculture also enjoys the attention and support of international donors (such as USAID, the EU, and UNDP), which provide grants to nonprofit organizations and government partnerships.

The sector is characterized by low labor productivity and efficiency. Some of the conditions contributing to this situation are the lack of knowledge and experience, the lack of an entrepreneurial mindset among farmers, the lack of innovation, and the gaps in value chains.

Tamta Mamulaidze, CEO of Agronavti, said her company has started developing its product to address the evident needs in the agriculture sector by supporting farmers with an app that can combine information and data with access to markets. However, there is resistance to adopting new technology, and digital literacy among the rural population is low. Client (farmer) skepticism is particularly difficult to overcome, as startups cannot yet show proof of concept in the early stages. Mamulaidze mentions that building a revenue model around an agritech product could also be a challenge, as potential customers are used to receiving services for free through grants or with government subsidies. Because farmers lack a commercial orientation, they are not interested in adopting new technologies.

In terms of agricultural enterprises, startups working on hardware solutions (e.g., Farco) compete with large international players whose products are tested and proven, offer complementary services, and can be directly imported by these farmers and entrepreneurs, even if the price is higher. In this regard, Georgian agritech startups lack competitive advantages and product innovation.

There is a need to rejuvenate the industry and attract young people. Vocational training in agriculture is gradually developing with the support of public–private partnerships and international donors. For example, the Agricultural University of Georgia (which was renovated in 2012) is trying to provide the sector with a skilled workforce. However, there is still room for including technological education and know-how in the curriculum. Tamta Mamulaidze of Agronavti said that "a marriage of agricultural and technical knowledge is critical."

> "Regardless of how well you work with tech and how entrepreneurial your mindset is, you need to have industry expertise and agronomic grounding to base business decisions on."
>
> *(Tamta Mamulaidze, CEO of Agronavti)*

While there are donor-funded programs and competitions to encourage young people to develop innovative solutions for agriculture, there are no venues for agritech enthusiasts to try and test new approaches, share knowledge, and develop prototypes. Furthermore, one-off projects and competitions do not support the development of startups, as they are short-term, mostly student-focused activities that do not provide significant financial or technical support for startups. Efforts need to be scaled-up and diversified to address different needs at different startup stages beyond ideation, including providing funding and capacity building.

Finally, the meaning of the word "agriculture" in Georgian may reduce young people's interest in the sector. The word means "village work" or "village production." This meaning limits understanding of what agriculture or agritech might be and where it is practiced. While many startup founders and other industry advocates use the words "agro" or "agro-production" as alternatives, the original meaning is commonly used (even in the name of the Ministry of Agriculture). Tusia Gharibashvili, cofounder of SpaceFarms and founder of Spots modular farming, an automated vertical urban farm, believes that such subtle details shape society's understanding of the industry and create a misconception, especially among the younger generation, that agricultural activities take place only in villages, where there is a traditional lack of innovation or technological development.

Overall, there is significant potential to modernize the sector through the introduction of new technologies, while creating opportunities for startups to experiment with and introduce new approaches to farming. In other countries, innovative approaches such as automated farming systems, vertical farming, and aeroponics are important innovations that Georgian startups could introduce or develop. Currently, there is a lack of support for agritech (e.g., lack of tailored programs and funding for startups or incentives for farmers to adopt technologies offered by startups).

However, there are positive developments as more initiatives are being introduced to get young people interested in agritech through ideation competitions and hackathons run by local organizations such as the Georgian Farmers' Association, Impact Hub Tbilisi, and Startup Büro, which are supported mainly by international donors, including UNDP and USAID. While these programs are increasing interest and awareness in the agritech sector as a whole, it is too early to tell how sustainable or effective these small and unique initiatives will be and whether they could actually help agritech startups emerge and grow.

Edtech

There is a growing demand for new and engaging ways to deliver education, including gamification, AI components, and multimedia programs for self-learning. More and more children are growing up as digital citizens, and with their parents, are looking for useful and safe online activities.

Nationwide, there are more than 2,300 accredited general education schools (grades 1–12), 91% of which are government-run. The number of students in these grades is about 624,500.[14] The number of government-owned universities is 101, and there are also 58 private universities. The number of university students in various programs and degrees is 76,000 at public universities and 21,000 at private universities.[15] The government's educational management information system oversees the use of digital tools by government schools in teaching. Although administrators and educators at public schools and universities have the option of using additional tools, they do not have control over their institution's digital infrastructure and base software, which is determined by the Ministry of Education and Science. Private institutions, on the other hand, determine their own digital infrastructure and use of tools.

Since the government is a major provider and developer of technology solutions, it poses a challenge to edtech startups offering products for school administrators, teachers, or students. The government usually approves and supplies international brands (e.g., Microsoft, Zoom, Moodle) or provides custom solutions developed internally at the educational management information system. The startups

---

[14] National Statistics Office of Georgia (GEOSTAT). General Education Statistics.
[15] GEOSTAT. Higher Education Statistics.

interviewed mentioned that even when tenders are announced, they are not designed to support startups, but are mostly tailored to typical software development companies that view this as a one-time software development order that does not result in the creation of a stand-alone project for wide market sale. SchoolBook, for example, was the first learning management system for general education schools in Georgia when it was established in 2013. It currently serves about 100 private schools. It also served more than 20 public schools (with an increasing trend) but had to terminate partnerships as the government decided to offer schools its own platform developed by another company. According to Irakli Kashibadze, founder of edtech startup GoandGrow and former head of GITA, the education market for digital solutions should be democratized and open to startups.

> "Similar to the way the banking sector has given space to fintech startups to emerge and use existing resources, the education sector should also be welcoming to startups."
>
> *(Irakli Kashibadze, founder of GoandGrow)*

Most edtech platforms in Georgia are tailored to the domestic education system. It is sometimes difficult for startups to adapt because education reforms are frequent and unpredictable, making their validated products or business models outdated. Furthermore, most startups are designed for Georgian-speaking users, and translating products into other languages for use outside the country requires significant investment and adaptation. Platforms designed for schoolchildren must be based on the purchasing power and willingness of parents to sign up for them. In Georgia, parents are not accustomed to paying for digital education services. For example, they are more willing to pay for a personal tutor than an AI-powered digital learning assistant.

Despite the challenges described above, the coronavirus disease (COVID-19) pandemic has accelerated the adoption of digital tools by educators, educational institutions, students, and parents in Georgia. Private schools and universities in Georgia have been more likely to adopt new technologies and are not constrained by government procurement or other guidelines. Compared with public schools, which are free to students, tuition-based institutions have a greater incentive to improve learning by offering students a quality learning experience.

The government could be a key player in encouraging the adoption of edtech products, as it operates most of the schools in the country. In addition, Georgian startups do not have to limit themselves to the domestic market but can target foreign markets. Edtech startups can cover a wide range of teaching, learning, and administrative functions. EduPay, for example, is a Georgian fintech platform for educational and other institutions that helps both administrators and students (or their parents) pay, receive, and manage tuition. The company was launched in 2021 and currently serves a dozen institutions, including private schools and sports clubs.

Cleantech

Many of the world's most successful startups are in the software business. Such startups often use software to replace labor and thereby generate cost savings for their clients. In contrast, cleantech companies develop solutions that initially come at a high cost to their clients (because the solutions help clients adhere to environmental regulations). Cleantech startups are not typical garage-based initiatives and require far more industry expertise, time, and patient capital than digital-based startups. According to a recent report by Startup Genome (2022), cleantech startups may face significant barriers in global markets, compete with large companies, and deal with complicated legal and environmental regulations. Over the years, venture capitalists or large corporations have invested heavily in cleantech, and the field continues to gain traction as environmental awareness increases worldwide. The biggest challenge for cleantech startups is scale-up. Globally, cleantech companies take the most time to move through stages of funding, with the average company taking 3.8 years to reach Series A and 5.5 years to reach Series B funding—almost 8 months and 11 months longer, respectively, than the average tech startup (Startup Genome 2022).

In Georgia, the cleantech sector is the least developed of the four sectors. Environmental issues are not a high priority for the country, and there is no targeted support for cleantech startups. Available support is focused on large infrastructure projects and large, established companies. Globally, there is growing interest in the transition to green and clean energy. However, in Georgia, there is a lack of overall cleantech awareness and expertise. Consumer behavior and preferences are generally not focused on clean energy and environmental solutions. Some cleantech experts point out that demand-side policies are needed to promote the industry. Additionally, venture capitalists, governments, and development foundations should join forces to provide larger and more patient capital options for cleantech startups. Global expertise could be matched with potential Georgian founders in the cleantech sector (Startup Genome 2022).

One of the most advanced cleantech companies in the country is BIOCURE. Its patented technology is used to isolate indigenous, oil-oxidizing bacterial cultures from spill sites. The company's technology is based on scientific research and experimentation that began in the 1990s. Only since 2017 has the company taken steps to advance its commercial growth. Similar to cleantech startups in other countries, BIOCURE's challenge is scaling up. Its operations must be tailored to the characteristics of each spill site and requires a large amount of labor. Its team is constantly looking for operational processes that can be replicated in other countries and a partnership model to expand operations globally.

BioDiesel is a startup that produces environmentally friendly fuel from new and used cooking oil. Its biodiesel plant has processed nearly 1 million liters of used cooking oil and produced more than 500 tons of clean biodiesel that is in demand in Europe. CEO Murman Pertaia said the company was able to sell 99% of its output to EU countries during the pandemic. "We have strong partners in the Netherlands, Bulgaria, and Portugal," he said.

Other startups such as Eco-Taxi (online platform to order pickup of recyclable materials from homes or offices) and Enovus (installation of clean energy solutions for residential or corporate buildings), are working with individual and corporate customers to change behavior toward recycling and green energy. However, none of these companies has developed a unique product that could be scaled up globally.

Healthtech

The global market for healthtech is growing and is expected to reach $660 billion by 2025 (Statista 2022). The pandemic and consequent restrictions for physical interaction have led more healthcare providers and patients to shift to telemedicine, which is the use of technology to deliver care remotely. Georgia digital health startups RedMed and Ekimo emerged at this time.

Entering the healthcare industry is not easy for most startups, as it requires industry knowledge, understanding of regulations, access to networks, and trust. RedMed's CEO, Tamara Metivishvili, explained that healthtech startups need to have not only technical skills in software development, but also good operational processes and a solid team to handle the complexity of the industry, including service delivery.

The healthtech market in Georgia is driven by subsidiaries of large corporations and insurance companies that already have a solid base in the healthcare industry (Ekimo, RedMed) and have access to stable startup funding and human resources through their principal companies. In comparison, MyDoc, a startup with a similar product founded years earlier by an experienced tech team, has not been as successful in securing large-scale partnerships with medical providers and creating customer traction. Compared with the competitors mentioned above, the company did not invest significant resources in marketing efforts.

Overall, all startups in the industry face a lack of patient trust in digital healthcare services, as these services are still new.

"We are still used to sitting across from a doctor, face-to-face, while in reality 90% of primary healthcare does not require a physical visit."

(Monika Kobuladze, former CEO of Ekimo)

Monika Kobuladze, former CEO of Ekimo, also mentioned that there is a large customer segment that is not digitally savvy and not able to use such services, especially the rural population and the elderly. Healthcare facilities and doctors also sometimes resist adopting new technologies because the process of adoption takes time and effort. As for the technical integration of the healthcare providers with the startup's product, some facilities use their own digital calendars and other patient-related systems so integration must be tailored and cannot be standardized. Additionally, some healthcare providers prefer to develop their own apps and services rather than adopt a third-party solution.

In terms of legal requirements, online medical consultations are not directly supported (or rejected) by national legislation, as having equal authority as face-to-face consultations. The pandemic has helped make the remote consultations more commonplace, but the founders mention that clear definitions and regulations are needed for the healthtech industry.

In addition to digital health services, teams seeking to develop healthcare devices require intensive R&D and face difficulty obtaining funding. R&D also requires highly skilled expertise that is hard to find among enthusiastic students or young entrepreneurs and instead requires strategic partnerships with research institutions, relevant government agencies, or the private sector.

Stimulating Spaces, Incubators, and Accelerators

Startup ecosystems must provide entrepreneurs with access to relevant communities and business circles, tech spaces to develop product prototypes, incubators to accelerate growth, and business mentors. Georgia's startup landscape is still young, but many spaces, programs, and groups have already emerged.

Government-Supported and University Spaces

The government, particularly through GITA and supported by the GENIE program, has been a major contributor in creating spaces for prototyping and collaboration for young entrepreneurs by setting up fabrication laboratories (fablabs), innovation centers, and tech parks. With EU support, Tbilisi City Hall has opened the Spark Incubator, where young entrepreneurs receive training and mentoring. The Rustavi City Hall, in partnership with UNDP, launched the Rustavi Innovation Center to provide a space for young people to meet, develop ideas, and work on startups that address social challenges.

In addition, GITA provides funding to universities to establish labs where students learn digital skills and entrepreneurship is encouraged. These include the Knowledge Transfer and Innovation Center at Ivane Javakhishvili Tbilisi State University, GeoLab at Georgian American University, and UniLab at Ilia State University. There are also several private university-based spaces and programs. The Startup Factory at the University of Georgia provides training and mentoring. The Business and Technology University has established an Entrepreneurship Center that offers several support programs, including a pre-accelerator in partnership with the European Fund for Southeast Europe (EFSE). Startups receive mentoring for 3 weeks and compete for a grant of up to GEL10,000 on demonstration (demo) day.

Most of these programs have been established in the last 5 years (Appendix 5). However, consistency, continuity, and scalability remain challenges. Most programs are ad hoc one-offs and lack long-term planning and coordination among institutions. Different stakeholders have different ideas about startups, entrepreneurial education, and the support processes needed.

Communities, Nonprofit Organizations, and Collaborative Spaces

Technology and startup communities have flourished in Georgia, providing opportunities for entrepreneurship education, networking, and startup growth. There are nonprofit organizations, advocacy groups, and companies such as ICT Cluster that bring together and advocate for technology companies. Startup Büro, for example, supports the development of entrepreneurial culture through various events and conferences. Impact Hub Tbilisi, a member of the global Impact Hub network, opened in Georgia in 2017 and offers coworking spaces and various programs for technology specialists and startups. Terminal is a local brand of coworking spaces with five locations across the country. Startups describe such spaces as helpful for meeting like-minded technology enthusiasts, entrepreneurs, or other startup teams. Another way for founders to network is through Startup Grind. This is a global movement, supported by Google, whose local organizers hold regular fireside chats with established entrepreneurs and investors from Georgia and other countries (mostly the US).

In addition, the technology and startup communities connect online and in person through events and conferences in groups such as Startup Info, Touch, Data Science Tbilisi, Google Developer Groups, Women Techmakers, and others. As well, Startup Büro has created a digital map of the local ecosystem that provides information on tech startups, coworking and maker spaces, meetup groups, incubator and accelerator programs, nonprofit organizations, and others.[16]

[16]   Startup Büro. Map of Georgia's Tech-Startup Ecosystem.

Based on interviews and observations, existing organizations, spaces, and communities have impacted the local ecosystem. However, many of them struggle to provide consistent programming because they depend on donations or rely on volunteers. Such initiatives could be strengthened if they had access to core institutional funding, rather than the activity- and project-based funding currently available. This could help community leaders and organizers be more flexible and tailor their events or operating models to the specific needs of the community.

Startup Incubators and Accelerators

Incubator and accelerator programs are an integral part of most startup ecosystems providing startups with infrastructure, support and training, and other elements of the ecosystem that support startups that might otherwise feel isolated. A highlight in recent years was the entry of 500 Startups with the help of GITA and Bank of Georgia. 500 Startups is a well-known early-stage venture fund and seed accelerator headquartered in the US. In Georgia, it has supported 30 startups with acceleration training and mentoring since 2019. Among them were two agritech startups, one of which was Agronavti, covered in this report. The English-language program is open to startups in Georgia and neighboring countries. The program uses lecturers and mentors from Silicon Valley, organizes final demo days, and supports startups with international business connections. After two successful batches, the GEL17.5 million contract was signed between GITA and 500 Global, which will cover the cost of incubation and training of eight batches of startups over the next 4 years (potentially 120 startups).

In addition, Bank of Georgia will continue to provide equity to the startups selected under the incubator program. The initial pilot program of 500 Startups in Georgia allowed selected ecosystem players to observe the incubation process so that these players could create or improve their own programs. Grants were also awarded for new programs. Business and Technology University and Impact Hub received such support to create programs. Pre-accelerators provide a crash course toward accelerator readiness. Through the pre-accelerators, startups that may only have an idea or are still in the prototype phase become better equipped (ahead in product and customer development) and ready to participate in local or global incubators and accelerator programs. Impact Hub Tbilisi organized its first Startup Pre-Accelerator in 2021 with 20 early-stage technology startups (one agritech, two edtech, and one healthtech). In 2022, 40 startups will participate in the program. The program is supported by EFSE and TBC Bank. The program does not provide direct funding to the startups.

Another recent initiative is the Redberry Startup Studio, a local incubator supported by private equity funds. It is run by the digital agency Redberry and backed by $3.2 million from Georgia Capital, a large investment firm. The incubator describes itself as a "Swiss army knife" for startup founders, offering them business and marketing training, mentors, funding of up to GEL160,000, and business development and marketing support. In return, Redberry takes an equity stake of up to 40%. The studio is still young and has only produced a few startups, none of which fall into the four focus areas of this report. The incubator supports primarily on SaaS and B2B solutions, but all types of startups can apply.

The GREENcubator, managed by the Caucasus Environmental NGO Network and Startup Büro, supports green initiatives, especially for specific demographic groups (women, minorities, etc.). However, the focus is on traditional solutions rather than those that use innovative technologies. In addition, Future Laboratory (a local innovation consulting firm) and Toyota launched Startup Drive in 2022—a competition for startups working on clean transportation solutions, road safety, navigation, ICT systems, and other areas of the automobile industry and transportation industries. Selected startups will receive a grant of GEL5,000 to work on a prototype and participate in a 3-month accelerator program. Selected teams will present at demo day and compete for an investment of up to GEL200,000.

Table 3: Startup Incubator and Accelerator Programs in Georgia

Program Name	Implementers, Sponsors, and Partners	No. of Startups Served	Scope	Funding and Equity	Frequency
500 Startups Georgia (Duration: 4 months)	Bank of Georgia, Georgia's Innovation and Technology Agency (GITA)	30 in 2 batches	Equity financing, training, practical assignments, international mentors, demo day, shadows program	Up to GEL330,000 and up to 10% equity	Batch intake annually, the possibility of next batches yet not confirmed
Redberry Startup Studio (Duration: 11 weeks; up to 12 months startup studio program)	Redberry, Georgia Capital	7 across rolling bases	Equity financing, training, mentors, involvement in business development and marketing	Up to GEL160,000 and up to 40% equity	Rolling basis
Impact Hub Pre-Accelerator (Duration: 4 months; in addition, for top five startups 6 months membership and coworking space at Impact Hub)	Impact Hub Tbilisi, European Fund for Southeast Europe (EFSE), GITA, Redberry, The Embassy of the Netherlands in Georgia	20 in 1 batch	Training, practical assignments, mentors, demo day shadows program	None; support to apply for GITA's grants; introduction to potential investors	One-off grant program, possibility of extension to two more batches
BTU Pre-Accelerator (Duration: 3 weeks)	Business and Technology University, EFSE, GITA	28 in 1 batch	Training, mentors, demo day	Up to GEL10,000 grant, no equity	One-off grant program, no follow up planned

continued on next page

Table 3 *continued*

Program Name	Implementers, Sponsors, and Partners	No. of Startups Served	Scope	Funding and Equity	Frequency
UG Startup Factory (Duration: 2 months)	University of Georgia	90 in 6 batches	Training, mentors, office hours demo day	None; support to apply for GITA's grants	Annually
GREENcubator (Duration: 3 weeks)	CENN, Startup Büro	30 in 1 batch	Training, mentors	None; potential to continue collaboration with CENN	One-off grant program, no follow up planned
Social Impact Award (Duration: 2 months)	Impact Hub Tbilisi, UNDP, TBC Startuper, and others	50 in 5 batches	Training, mentors, demo day	Up to GEL7,000 grant, no equity; possibility to attend Global Summit	Annually, based on support of local sponsors and partners
Startup Drive (Duration: 3 months)	Toyota Georgia, Future Laboratory	10 in 1 batch	Training, mentors, demo day, investment	Up to GEL200,000 investment fund (might be divided among up to 5 startups)	One-off initiative, no information on planned replication

Source: Authors, based on interviews and data from official websites.

Incubators and accelerator programs are still relatively new in Georgia. Of the startups interviewed, only a few had participated in them. Those that had participated emphasized that they had a significant impact on product and customer development and contact with potential partners and investors. They helped founders improve their understanding of how to run a startup, including aspects of fundraising. This sentiment was also expressed for programs that did not provide grants or equity investments, but helped founders tap into investor networks through demo days and other means. Giorgi Khachidze, CEO of EduPay, said that after a 3-month program, the Impact Hub Tbilisi's accelerator helped take their idea and operation of the company to the next level.

> "We were ready as never [before] to talk to investors, gain funds and understand what our strategic approaches should be for growth. The exposure and connections brought us valuable partners and business customers, as well as lifelong mentors."
>
> *(Giorgi Khachidze, CEO of EduPay)*

Tamta Mamulaishvili, CEO of Agronavti, said that participating in 500 Startups' accelerator was an exceptional opportunity. The company was able to reevaluate the features of its existing product and develop data-driven solutions. Those startups that received a GITA grant of GEL100,000 also received access to a short accelerator training course. The sample size of these interviews is too small to draw generalized conclusions, but they suggest a pattern: startups that were exposed to structured and longer training and mentoring made significant progress in product development and market validation.

In summary, several accelerator and incubator programs have been launched in the country. Some of these may have had a lasting impact on the ecosystem. However, most of them are one-off projects that will not be replicated. A key reason for these ad hoc projects is the lack of access to stable and sustainable funding and a reliance on donor funding for initiatives of short duration. For each iteration, they have to go through a fundraising process and convince stakeholders, which takes time and effort and can curb enthusiasm. Incubator and accelerator managers struggle to find a profitable business model for operations. None of the programs charge participation fees and providing a share of equity to the program is rarely a requirement for a participating startup. Even when an incubator asks a startup to give up some equity in exchange for incubation services (e.g., Redberry Startup Studio), that equity cannot be easily liquidated and used to cover the incubator's operating costs. For incubator or accelerator programs to become self-sustaining, they should consider revenue-generating mechanisms, such as charging fees or implementing other systems that allow them to run ongoing programs without financial constraints.

In addition to local programs, it is important to note that there are cases of Georgian startups participating in incubator programs in Europe or the US, including the competitive accelerators of TechStars and Y Combinator. Such programs provide Georgian startups with valuable opportunity to expand their networks, meet potential investors, and equip themselves with advanced knowledge and expertise. However, not many Georgian startups are able to participate in such international programs as most startups' maturity level is still low. Therefore, local programs such as the aforementioned pre-accelerators and incubators are important to help startups gain a foundation of knowledge and business growth, and that might help to prepare for participation in international programs.

Human Capital

Overview

Human capital is at the heart of the startup ecosystem. Tech talent and entrepreneurs who are competent, courageous, and have a business mindset are key assets to the system. They harness opportunities and create innovative solutions that they seek to implement at scale. Creating a startup requires a combination of skill, passion, and risk-taking. Georgia has a relatively short history of free markets and a shallow entrepreneurship culture. Tech startups have only emerged in the last decade, although their numbers are growing. For the country's startup ecosystem to thrive, significant improvements in education, skills, and talent development are needed (UNECE 2020).

Georgia has recently made tremendous improvements in education participation and learning outcomes (OECD 2019). In 2004, Georgia introduced comprehensive reforms at all levels of education with the goal of creating a credible education system that provides learning according to international standards. Substantial international donor funding has been allocated to ongoing education reforms and to support the Socioeconomic Development Strategy, known as Georgia 2020. Public spending on education has increased and amounted to 3.9% of GDP in 2020. The same metric for the EU averaged 4.6% in 2018.[17]

The Global Competitiveness Report ranks Georgia low in terms of social capital (i.e., collaboration, networking), graduates' skills, and quality of vocational education (WEF 2019). The World Bank's Human Capital Index (HCI) has an overall HCI score of 0.57, meaning that a child born in Georgia is expected to be 57% as productive as if they enjoyed a quality education and full health. Georgia's HCI score for 2020 is above the average for upper middle-income countries worldwide, although it is below the average for countries in Europe and Central Asia. Improving the quality of education, as reflected in international test scores, would help Georgia catch up with the regional average (World Bank 2020b).

In 2019, the European Union launched a 5-year €50 million program called Skills4Jobs to improve the skills of the country's workforce. Currently, the World Bank is supporting two key human capital development projects: the Innovation, Inclusion and Quality project, to improve access to preschool education, increase the quality of education, and strengthen the learning environment; and the Log-in Georgia project, to provide fast and affordable broadband internet connectivity to nearly 500,000 people in rural and remote areas to enable e-learning and telemedicine, both of which were important during the COVID-19 pandemic.

Technology Competence

Georgia ranked eighth to last out of 79 countries in the 2018 Programme for International Student Assessment in reading, mathematics, and science. Georgia was well below the Organisation for Economic Co-operation and Development average in all three competencies. In Georgia, socioeconomically advantaged students perform better in reading than disadvantaged students (OECD 2018).

Student performance and the distribution of the skilled workforce are unequal across the country, primarily due to weaknesses in schooling in rural areas and disadvantaged communities, particularly in technological knowledge and soft skills. A disparity also exists between public and private schools, with private

---

17   World Bank. World Development Indicators. Government Expenditure on Education, total (% of GDP) – Georgia and Government Expenditure on Education, total (% of GDP) – European Union.

schools better able to adapt to changing labor dynamics and offer a more diversified curriculum, including higher quality science, technology, engineering, and mathematics (STEM) and entrepreneurship training.

Undergraduate (BA) and graduate (MA) programs offered by universities do not match current market needs (USAID Georgia 2017). Informal and self-paced education programs may be more effective in teaching essential skills in some cases. Recently, government, private companies, and training centers have increasingly offered short courses in IT and software development (Appendix 6). In 2013, the Millennium Challenge Corporation and the government signed a $140 million agreement to improve STEM education. The initiative included school-level programs, improvements to technical and vocational education and training, a partnership between the University of San Diego and Georgian universities to develop joint programs and improve the quality of skilled STEM workers, and programs to empower women and reduce poverty. Recently, Kutaisi International University was established and offers degree programs in computer science, mathematics, and management, as well as postgraduate programs in finance and information management. It has an international orientation and links with institutions abroad. The school welcomed its first students in 2021. The school emphasizes the importance of scientific research and entrepreneurial education.

In 2018, GITA completed an ICT labor market analysis to identify the need for a digitally skilled workforce to meet the requirements of the domestic and international markets. It then began implementing a collaborative skills program consisting of ICT training courses with international exams to improve digital skills in line with the country's economic and digital strategies. The program aims to train and certify 3,000 citizens by mid-2023. GITA also plans to offer a basic digital skills training program for 5,000 beginners in 2022–2024.

In the EBRD's Business Environment and Enterprise Performance Survey, the lack of innovation-specific management skills was cited as one of the main challenges preventing Georgian companies from collaborating with foreign and domestic knowledge partners, investing in R&D, and innovating in general (EBRD 2017). Startups compete with large companies for scarce tech talent and have difficulty finding skilled workers because startups cannot pay high salaries and are a riskier employer. Producing creative and high-quality products and participating in international value chains becomes difficult without a skilled workforce.

R&D is critical to startups in the four focused sectors in the report. Georgia's gross expenditure on R&D has increased in recent years, but it is still seven times lower than the recommended EU spending of 3% of GDP (USAID Georgia 2017). Georgian companies invest little in innovation, collaboration between scientific circles and industry is limited, and the competence and scope of research institutions requires improvement (UNECE 2020). The government created the Research in Innovation Council in 2015, but it ceased operations shortly after its creation. Through the government's Shota Rustaveli National Science Foundation, universities can apply for research grants, but the amount of funding is limited, and the terms and conditions are sometimes difficult for universities to meet. GITA, the World Bank, Experts.ai, and the Knowledge Transfer and Innovation Center of Ivane Javakhishvili Tbilisi State University have been working on the commercialization of science, but significant results have yet to be achieved. The low level of industrial research and innovation is also due to a mismatch between scientific knowledge and industry understanding (i.e., a business mindset within academia). Additional seed financing and strategic collaboration with industry are needed to further expand applied research at Georgian scientific institutions.

> "We see young entrepreneurs who are eager to come up with innovative solutions, and we see senior scientists who have the competence. But the problem is that they hardly come together to collaborate."
>
> *(Khatuna Sandroshvili, program manager of UNDP Georgia)*

The challenge of finding qualified tech professionals was frequently cited by startups and stakeholders. Overall, there is intense competition for tech talent between banks and software development companies, including international companies such as EPAM and Exatel, which have recently entered the market and offer attractive conditions to new employees.

Remote work has always been an opportunity for ICT professions. The pandemic has made it even more appealing. As a result, many Georgian tech experts work remotely for foreign companies (mainly in the US and Europe). Generally, Georgian tech professionals earn a high income, especially if they are hired by international companies in or outside Georgia. In this competitive environment, it is difficult for startups to recruit team members as they cannot offer high salaries and do not have bonus systems in the initial stages. The hardest professionals to find for software-related startups are mobile app developers and data scientists. For agritech, cleantech, and healthtech startups, it is difficult to find talent that combines industry knowledge and digital expertise. Another in-demand professional for startups are marketing and business development managers who understand startups' characteristics and can lead data-driven growth marketing efforts.

Almost no startups are looking for engineers or IT personnel outside of Georgia to work remotely. This option has not been discussed or considered. While some startups are in contact with career offices, there are no streamlined processes or procedures for startups to access up-and-coming young talent through universities. Recruitment is usually through word-of-mouth and personal contacts, especially for early-stage startups. Some startups have unstructured training procedures to hire newcomers, especially university graduates. But such practices are rare, especially for early-stage startups, as they do not have the time or administrative resources to invest in training.

In 2021, Skills Agency Georgia was established as a public–private partnership by the government and the Georgia Chamber of Commerce and Industry. The main goal of Skills Agency Georgia is to develop a flexible vocational education system through a public–private partnership to provide high-quality skills training that is relevant to employers and based on effective communication between industry and the workforce. One of the agency's priorities will be digital skills training. The agency will support sectoral skills organizations and professional associations and provide incentives for these entities to collaborate across sectors.

Entrepreneurial Mindset and Startup Foundership

Establishing innovative companies requires an entrepreneurial mindset among founders and throughout the ecosystem. Georgians' positive perceptions about entrepreneurship are below global and regional averages (GEM 2016). These perceptions relate to both recognizing opportunities and personal capabilities, as well as actual entrepreneurial intentions. Additionally, a survey by the Global Entrepreneurship Monitor found that of those who see opportunities for entrepreneurial activity in Georgia, 30.7% of women and 16.7% of men are afraid of failure, which may deter them from starting a business (GEM 2014). Although more than 80% of the population aged 18 to 65 see entrepreneurship as a good career option or a way to gain status, motivation to become an entrepreneur is low (GEM 2016). This may be due to the low self-confidence mentioned earlier. The right entrepreneurial education and access to social capital can strengthen or weaken self-confidence and the willingness to start one's own business. Therefore, these two factors need to be strengthened to motivate people to become entrepreneurs.

Georgia is a fairly young country in terms of free market economy, not to mention the startup scene, which is even more nascent. The lack of role models and business talent know-how is still an obstacle. Nevertheless, creating a startup is becoming more popular among young people, and there are already examples of successful tech companies in the country. Most startups are based in Tbilisi, reflecting the general social and economic disparities in the country, as most activities are concentrated in the capital. Other major cities such as Rustavi, Kutaisi, and Batumi are potential areas for a startup ecosystem, as they have considerable economic activity and access to tech talent (e.g., universities in Batumi and Kutaisi that teach software development).

Demographically, the average age of startup founders, especially the more established startups, is over 30. Most of the founders have a postgraduate degree (master's degree). There are examples of Georgian returnees from abroad or expats creating startups, but this trend is not common. There is a lack of female startup founders. This was the case in all sectors from which startups were interviewed except agritech, where most established startups are headed by women. However, of all the startups interviewed, only one had a female tech cofounder. The lack of female business owners (22%) and female top managers (16%) is a nationwide feature across all sectors (World Bank 2019). For startups, the lack of female founders could be due to socioeconomic factors, such as an overall lower risk appetite and preference for stable salaries; lack of savings and property to back up the bootstrapping process with cash or collateral required for banks; general gender roles due to women's traditional position in society; lack of role models, with "businessman" being a typical term for someone who runs a business; gender disparities in ICT professions leading to a low number of female tech founders; and lack of social capital and engagement in professional business circles.

It is interesting to observe how much intrapreneurship is taking place in Georgian businesses. Although the overall human capital index or entrepreneurial intentions may be low, there appears to be a critical mass of workers involved in corporate life who have a high work ethic, competence, and international experience. In Georgia, many of the most successful companies were founded by individuals who left the corporate world or innovated within their own company by creating a subsidiary. Therefore, supporting intrapreneurship and spin-offs from existing tech or non-tech companies could be one of the paths forward for Georgia.

A large proportion of the startups interviewed, especially those that managed to get past the prototype stage and enter the market, were cofounded by another company with expertise in the same sector such as healthcare (RedMed, Ekimo), agriculture (Agronavti, SpaceFarms), education (Murtsku, TV School, Lupi, GoandGrow, Lingwing), or ICT and software development (Nebula, MyDoc). Such companies are better able to overcome challenges, especially in accessing finance, hiring employees, acquiring customers, and building partnerships. Founders with previous startup or entrepreneurial experience, or those supported by other companies, are more likely to move quicker toward commercialization, while first-time founders tend to be more idea-oriented and focused on technology, with some also driven to achieving social goals.

According to the Harvard Business Review, companies whose employees have both business and technical skills are more likely to introduce new innovations to the marketplace than companies that have only one type of skill (Murmann 2017). Many of the startups interviewed for this study do not have tech expertise (e.g., a tech cofounder). For those whose founder is a tech expert, bootstrapping is easier because wages are not spent on tech talent. For startups without tech founders, finding such talent is challenging and hiring is costly.

The reasons for the low number of tech founders vary. It may be that software developers and other techies lack the entrepreneurial skills or interest in running a business. It may also be that a tech expert has a stable and well-paying job. In a country with a history of political and economic turmoil, losing a steady job and the income that comes with it is a big risk, and there is no guarantee of immediate profits from a startup. Additionally, agritech, cleantech, edtech, and healthtech may not be attractive or interesting to software developers and engineers, and they may be more interested in technology verticals such as blockchain or artificial intelligence.

For most founders, startups are a sideline to their paid jobs. As a result, founders' lack of time hinders startups from being active and quick to prototype, test, and pivot. Founders can rarely afford to quit their jobs and devote maximum time to their startups. The ability to support themselves and their families with savings while running a startup is rare. Even startups that have received grants from the government usually do not use that money to pay their own salaries, as most startups (especially those without tech founders) need to hire and pay employees. Startups that are cofounded by other companies have greater capacity to retain their founders or core team on a full-time paid basis and can therefore grow faster.

TBC Bank is implementing a program called Startup Leave that encourages its employees to create their own startups. Employees pitch their business ideas at a startup competition, and if selected, they can take a 6-month paid sabbatical to focus on their startup, while also receiving marketing support, visibility, and mentoring from the company's business and technology teams.

> "We want to foster an entrepreneurial culture within our company, so giving our employees the opportunity to be creative is vital. My recommendation is that other companies cultivate an entrepreneurial mindset in their organizations as well, as it can have a significant impact on the output and overall, on the country's performance."
>
> (Nika Kurdiani, deputy CEO of TBC)

Another example of intrapreneurial opportunity is the Redberry Startup Studio mentioned above, which offers employees the opportunity to generate ideas and become cofounders with the studio of new startups.

The composition of a founding team impacts the success of a startup as early as the idea stage. Even if the founders know the problem, they may not understand or research the full extent of the problem or target audience, so their solutions may not be commercially or technically feasible. Some of the startups drew inspiration from products that exist outside Georgia. A bottleneck for this approach is that the local market characteristics or the competitive landscape (e.g., availability of international alternatives) may not have been adequately considered.

Georgian founders' startup ideas are often product-based, i.e., they just want to create a new product or service, and do not think enough about creating a new company (i.e., business model) that can be profitable and generate traction. Hardware-based startups are created either by importing equipment directly (e.g., AgriCopter, Enovus, SpaceFarms) or by assembling imported components in Georgia to produce a product (Farco, NovelVision). ICT-based startups that have technical expertise among cofounders can create a product and test it in the market before taking further steps, which works well with the type of startups that want to employ an accelerated test-and-pivot mode. This is most commonly seen in edtech startups that offer information- and platform-based solutions, such as SchoolBook, Murtsku, EduPay, and Lupi.

Founders who start without technical expertise in the team first build visibility for their idea, secure grants, and then begin product development through hired employees or outsourced companies (e.g., Agronavti). This format presents a challenge for some startups because the product is not created just once in its final form but requires constant development and feature redesign based on customer validation. R&D-based startups, especially in the cleantech industry (e.g., BIOCURE, BioDiesel, BioChimPharm) go through product development cycles more so than ICT startups. The resources required to complete these cycles (including technical infrastructure, laboratories, money, and time) are much greater, and they require more industry-specific expertise.

In Georgia, it is not common to conduct thorough market research to determine the demand for a product. While startups use national statistics or data on what is happening outside of Georgia in specific sectors, they often lack an understanding of the local market. The availability of detailed, industry-specific reports and data on Georgia was cited as a challenge by startups. Where reports and data do exist, startups lack expertise in how to find them (including for the international market).

Markets—and the business models needed to access them—can vary among sectors. For example, startups in the agritech and cleantech sectors, based primarily on tangible products and hardware, have primarily B2B business models and seek revenue from larger orders and transactions (e.g., BioDiesel, BIOCURE, AgriCopter, Smart Aeroponics). B2B solutions in edtech are characterized by subscription-based approaches where unit costs are low and the focus is on scaling (e.g., SchoolBook, TV School, EduPay). Business-to-consumer-oriented startups seem to have more difficulty finding the best business model or pricing strategies.

This is especially true for consumers who are not used to paying for online services, such as farmers (Agronavti) or students and parents (Lupi, Nebula, Murtsku). Some of these platforms are moving toward making their platform freely accessible for users and using this traction as an asset that would be of interest to third parties through advertising (Facebook model) or other ways of accessing their target audiences. Creating an online marketplace of sorts is also an approach of startups in Georgia. For such platforms, a large number of users on both sides of the market (i.e., buyers and sellers) is crucial. Those that invested great effort in building these networks (e.g., Soplidan.ge) were able to capture the market and grow, while others that focused only on the product and did not pursue the marketing element ran into difficulties (e.g., MyDoc.chat).

While most startups use standard business and revenue models (direct product or service sales, subscription, transaction commissions), there are rare but positive signs of business model innovation. A good example is SpaceFarms, which is not just selling "greens" (i.e., vegetables) from its urban vertical farm to its B2B clients (stores, hotels) but plans to create new, remote-controlled potting devices to be placed in these venues. SpaceFarms would "rent" 1–2 square meters from these venues to place the device on their space, and instead charge them a fee each time they use the greens harvested inside. With this approach, SpaceFarms can expand without a large infrastructure investment, grow 15 times more produce in vertical farm pots, and, most importantly, make freshly grown greens available to stores and hotels.

Startups with smaller teams and lack of financial resources have obvious gaps in product marketing and customer outreach. Founders may try to put on the hat of a marketing professional, but lack of knowledge and experience is a constraint. Startups backed by larger companies, especially in healthtech (RedMed, Ekimo), have sophisticated product marketing driven by outsourced professionals or in-house marketers to generate sales.

Most startups gain visibility by appearing on TV programs, especially if they participate in startup competitions or receive funding. The use of Facebook for business purposes is very common in Georgia, and startups interact with their potential or existing customers through Facebook. Entering the market and attracting initial customers and partners is usually done by word of mouth and is obviously easier for founders who already have industry contacts derived from work experience. Younger founders who lack social capital face challenges. Most startups that move beyond the prototype stage are already generating revenue. On average, startups that have achieved financial sustainability have been operating for more than 3 years. Startups that are cofounded or supported by other companies (BioChimPharm, Nebula, MyDoc.chat) or founders running multiple startups simultaneously (Murtsku, Lupi, TV School), are able to share resources and reduce costs.

Recommendations

A top priority for Georgia is to promote innovation and technological progress to increase the economy's competitiveness. The government has introduced policies and programs to support the development of the startups' ecosystem, and there has been considerable progress in improving the business climate in recent decades. However, entrepreneurs still struggle to generate innovation, to gain access to finance, and to build sustainable startups. Below are recommendations that can improve the system of support.

Stage of Development

Support should be tailored to the different stages of development—from early to mature. While startups in the idea and pre-seed stages need access to general mentoring and business growth, more mature startups in the growth stage require support to achieve product-market fit and implement growth strategies for domestic and international expansion. Regarding finance, grants are a good "stimulator" in the early stages, but should not be seen as a long-term option. Instead, startups should be supported in graduating to other forms of financing, such as venture capital, as they grow.

Tech startups should be distinguished from other small enterprises in terms of regulations, taxes, and programs. Startups are unique businesses where the early development of technology—without a revenue flow—presents challenges. Governments can offer tailored support and regulation. Tax incentives for tech startups could be provided, including reduced corporate, value-added, and income taxes for employees (the latter is currently available for employees of international digital companies in Georgia). Startups that produce hardware would benefit from reduced tariffs on technological components needed for prototyping in the early stages.

Finance

Grants are good, but deeper funding is required. Most of the funding for technology startups in Georgia is provided through government programs and focuses on grants for early-stage startups. However, grants are not sufficient to develop prototypes for sophisticated scientific solutions, especially in cleantech. In addition, donor support, often linked to the Sustainable Development Goals, is primarily project-based and does not fully meet the needs of startups.

Additional venture capital and angel investment—domestic and foreign— is needed. In general, founding teams and potential investors lack knowledge and experience with investing in startups. For their part, startups need to better understand the constraints and obligations associated with receiving outside investment and how to pitch for and negotiate funding deals.

Skills for fundraising and networking with investors can be improved. Many startups lack investment literacy, meaning they don't know how to approach investors and pitch or convince them to invest. Training and guidance on fundraising can be provided by incubator and accelerator programs, startup associations, or focused courses offered by public agencies supporting startups, such as GITA. Furthermore, a dense web of networking opportunities needs to be developed to connect startups with investors, notably venture capital funds and angel groups in and outside Georgia. This can be achieved by strengthening existing public–private initiatives in this area.

Sectors and Markets

Specific incentives are needed for agritech, cleantech, edtech, and healthtech. As in other countries, startup activity is concentrated in e-commerce, fintech, and digital platforms. Less attention is paid to sectors that have not only economic but also social and developmental impact. There are no direct policies or incentives to encourage startups in agritech, cleantech, edtech, and healthtech. Investors and funding sources do not prioritize startups in these areas.

Startups can target global markets. Startups need to recognize opportunities not only in the local market, but also in foreign or global markets. This requires knowledge-sharing and market access support. Partnerships with international institutions, the diaspora, and large companies can help. The technology scene in Georgia is growing and various SaaS, AI, and fintech solutions are becoming available. Agritech, cleantech, edtech, and healthtech are fast-growing global activities in which Georgia could secure a position if supported. Startups could leverage existing expertise in popular startup sectors to innovate in the four sectors. Examples include the use of AI in agriculture or fintech in education.

Agritech has great potential for growth in Georgia. The sector is of great importance to the economy and is currently supported by the government and donors in the development of agribusiness and community initiatives. There is a need to support the creation of more agritech startups and promote innovation and technology in the sector overall.

Women

Empower women as startup founders and lead managers. Men dominate the current startup landscape. Women can be empowered to establish startups through skills training, mentoring, gender-responsive funding opportunities, and other capacity-building activities. Awards can be given for the best female-led startup. Examples of successful women-led startups can be promoted and disseminated to serve as role models for other women who aspire to create a startup.

Innovation

Universities and innovation spaces can be an active resource for stimulating entrepreneurial interaction and startup creation. However, support is currently provided mainly at the idea stage. Startup accelerators with local and international mentors and a focus on product market validation are a very positive development that needs to be further encouraged. Opportunities are currently tailored to early-stage and pre-seed startups, and there is a lack of support for startups that need to grow their operations and expand their markets.

R&D and collaboration between young people and scientists through academic initiatives are beneficial. A combination of deep scientific knowledge and entrepreneurial know-how is particularly necessary for the emergence and growth of startups in agritech, cleantech, and healthtech. Universities could create more spaces and opportunities for young, tech- and digitally-savvy professionals to build connections with experienced scientists and industry experts in academia and the private sector. This could be achieved through longer-term initiatives such as innovation incubators, hackathons, and ideation competitions, where scientists and industry experts mentor students on product development and business initiation. These support mechanisms could also include providing patient capital for prototyping and testing (e.g., in collaboration with GITA as a major provider of startup grants and with support from industry corporations in agriculture, healthcare, and clean energy).

Talent

Prioritize human capital development for technology and innovation. An entrepreneurial and technologically creative mindset can be cultivated through government programs, universities, international academic partnerships, and collaboration with international donors. Tech startup training can be provided to professionals and students in a variety of disciplines, particularly agriculture, healthcare, environment, and education. It is important to incorporate technology competence, practical project-based learning, and entrepreneurial education into the education system to develop interest and knowledge among young people throughout the country, especially outside of Tbilisi. Programs should be inclusive to ensure equal access—and targeted initiatives—based on age, gender, location, and other criteria.

Georgia needs to improve its education system. Entrepreneurial experience and culture are also limited, so it is imperative to facilitate knowledge sharing and knowledge spillovers through domestic and international networks and partnerships. Startups in the cleantech, agritech, and healthtech sectors require more sophisticated, sector-specific expertise. Research and development capacity in Georgia is still limited, and synergies among scientists, young entrepreneurs, and other businesses, should be developed, supported by R&D funding. Despite Georgia's small population and overall low human capital, the country's large corporations have thousands of highly skilled employees and excellent managers. Consequently, there is a significant number of young workers who, if supported, can become entrepreneurs.

Address skills gaps in founding teams. Programs could target existing tech professionals and encourage them to better integrate into the startup ecosystem (e.g., through tech founderships or chief technology officer programs, tech stack discussions, networking initiatives, startup schools, and others). This could be achieved through a close partnership between stakeholders, such as GITA—a key player in the ecosystem, the tech industry itself, and organizations and universities that are already reaching thousands of people with their programs.

APPENDIXES

Appendix 1: List of Stakeholders Interviewed

No.	Organization	Type	Respondent
1	Georgia's Innovation and Technology Agency (GITA)	Government	Avtandil Kasradze, chairman
2	Business and Technology University (BTU)	Academia	Tako Japaridze, head of Entrepreneurship Center
3	500 Startups	Accelerator	Nato Chankvetadze, Georgia lead
4	Impact Hub Tbilisi	Private/Accelerator/Community	Ketevan Ebanoidze, cofounder
5	Redberry Startup Studio	Private sector/Venture capital (VC)	Gaga Darsalia, CEO
6	TBC Bank	Private sector	Nika Kurdiani, deputy CEO
7	Georgia Capital	VC	Giorgi Gureshidze, Water Utility and Renewable Energy Business
8	Startup Grind Georgia	Community	Colin M. Donohue, director
9	Startup Büro	Private sector	Guri Koiava, cofounder
10	Axel Investor Network	Angel network	Hayk Asriyants, cofounder
11	TSU Knowledge Transfer	Academia	Iro Tsagareishvili, main specialist
12	Rustavi Innovation Center	Nonprofit/Community	Revaz Barbakadze, head of Management
13	UNDP Georgia	Development organization	Khatuna Sandroshvili, program manager
14	Globalize	Private sector	Salome Kukava, founder and CEO

Appendix 2: List of Startups Interviewed

No.	Startup Name	Industry	Area of Work	Respondent
1	**Agronavti**	Agritech	App for farmers to gain information and access to markets	Tamta Mamulaidze, CEO
2	**Farco**	Agritech	Smart greenhouse solution	Ramaz Javakhishvili, CEO
3	**SpaceFarms**	Agritech	Fully automated urban vertical farming	Tusia Gharibashvili, CEO
4	**Smart Aeroponics**	Agritech	Aeroponics greenhouse management software	Onise Zivzivadze, CEO
5	**AgriCopter**	Agritech	Irrigation and crop protection via drones	Giorgi Danelia, CEO
6	Soplidan.ge	Agritech	Online marketplace for farm to table	Natia Ninikelashvili, CEO
7	**BioDiesel**	Cleantech	Produces bio diesel from new and used cooking oil	Murman Pataraia, CEO
8	**Eco-Taxi**	Cleantech	Waste management app to request pick-up of recycling materials	Mariam Pesvianidze and Tatiana Remneva, cofounders
9	**Enovus**	Cleantech	Modern energy efficiency and renewable energy startup, focused on enterprise solutions	Irakli Siradze, CEO
10	**BIOCURE**	Cleantech	Research and development to tackle oil pollution	Temo Rukhaia, CEO
11	**Lingwing**	Edtech	Language learning app similar to Duolingo	Vato Veliashvili, CEO
12	**SchoolBook**	Edtech	School management system, for administration and teachers	Lika Abramishvili, cofounder and COO
13	**Nebula**	Edtech	E-learning and exam preparation platform for high school students	Sandro Dolidze, cofounder
14	**GoandGrow**	Edtech	Professional development platform with courses, career support, etc.	Irakli Kashibadze, cofounder
15	**TV School**	Edtech	Platform for teachers to create and distribute homework assignments	Tamar Archvadze, project manager
16	**Lupi**	Edtech	Online learning platform for school students	
17	**Murtsku**	Edtech	Web platform to help students practice for exams and standardized tests	
18	**EduPay**	Edtech	Tuition systems for educational institutions	Giorgi Khachidze, CEO
19	**RedMed**	Healthtech	E-medicine app with online consultation	Tamara Metivishvili, CEO
20	**Ekimo**	Healthtech	E-medicine app with online consultation and pharmacy delivery	Monika Kobuladze, CEO, service director (former)

continued on next page

Appendix 2 *continued*

No.	Startup Name	Industry	Area of Work	Respondent
21	**MyDoc.chat**	Healthtech	Symptoms checking app with the possibility to consult with the doctor	Tornike Razmadze, cofounder, CTO
22	**BioChimPharm**	Healthtech	Biotechnological company engaged in research and development of medicine using natural phages	Rati Golijishvili, general manager
23	**NovelVision**	Healthtech	Adaptive devices for visually impaired	Nata Sulakvelidze, CEO, cofounder

Appendix 3: Government Financing Options for Technology Startups

Provider Institution	Maximum Amount (GEL)	Type	Required Cofinancing	Equity Take	Focus and Purpose	Frequency/ Availability
GITA	5,000	Grant	0%	0%	Founders and innovators, attendance at conferences, travel, professional growth programs	Rolling basis
GITA	15,000	Grant	0%	0%	Tech startups, prototyping	Rolling basis
GITA	100,000	Grant	10%	0%	Tech startups, product-market fit	Biannually
GITA	650,000	Grant	50%	0%	Tech startups, growth	Biannually
Enterprise Georgia	30,000	Grant	10% (5% if applicant is from a high mountain region)	0%	Support for micro and small businesses, no particular focus on technology Support is provided primarily for the establishment of enterprises that produce tangible goods (e.g., handicrafts, food, etc.) or provide services (e.g., tourism). A large part of the support is given to microentrepreneurs outside Tbilisi. Nonetheless, tech entrepreneurs can also apply, and there is anecdotal evidence of such cases.	Annually
Enterprise Georgia	1 million upon fulfillment of the investment obligation	Grant	GEL5 million	0%	Supports foreign direct investment projects, mostly for traditional industries. However, for business process outsourcing companies, the minimum investment is GEL5 million (~$1.5 million), with the creation of at least 200 new jobs.	Rolling basis
Startup Georgia	1 million	Investment	10%	Varied, no more than 55%	Innovative products and services. The applicant retains ownership of 45% of the equity, while the remaining portion may be distributed proportionally to Startup Georgia or other additional investors.	Rolling basis

continued on next page

Appendix 3 *continued*

Provider Institution	Maximum Amount (GEL)	Type	Required Cofinancing	Equity Take	Focus and Purpose	Frequency/ Availability
Zrda– Startup Georgia and USAID	1 million	Investment	10%	0%	It is not focused on technology and innovation. It targets entrepreneurs in conflict-affected border areas.	Rolling basis

Source: Authors, based on data provided by GITA, stakeholder interviews, and public information available on Georgia's Innovation and Technology Agency and Enterprise Georgia.

Appendix 4: List of Venture Capital Funds and Angel Investor Networks for Startups in Georgia

No.	Name	Description
1	**Angel Investor Club Georgia**	Invests $30,000–$200,000 in startups from idea stage to Series A funding rounds. Depending on the stage of the company being invested in, they participate in an equity funding round or provide either revenue-based funding or convertible debt. In addition to early-stage funding, they provide access to the network and expertise of club members, i.e., entrepreneurs and executives from blue-chip companies. During the fundraising process, they work with entrepreneurs to get them ready to invest. This includes helping them prepare investment documents and develop a pitch. Startups can apply directly through the angelinvestor.ge website. There is also a public membership inquiry form for interested investors to join the club. There are currently four founding members listed on the website.
2	**Axel – Georgian Business Angel Network**	Axel is a joint initiative of Startup Büro and Kedari Ventures. Kedari Ventures is a Georgian venture capital (VC) fund established to invest in and develop startups with scalable business models. Kedari's portfolio includes 15 companies. Startup Büro works closely with the private and public sectors to support the development of the technology and startup ecosystem through hackathons, business bootcamps, and events. There are currently 18 members listed on the website. Investors can express interest in joining the network through the axelnetwork.org website. Axel does not specify the amount of funding startups can apply for or the stage they must be at. Interested startups can apply for a pitching opportunity in front of the angel network via an online form.
3	**Cartooli**	Cartooli describes itself as a new kind of consulting firm, tailored to the needs and budgets of startups in emerging markets. Their initial focus is on supporting Georgian startups with growth potential. Their online platform features an extensive list of local startups (possibly the most comprehensive directory of active startups in the Georgian ecosystem) and a list of various international funding opportunities for Georgian founders as a tool to help raise an initial "friends and family" round by facilitating the creation of a special purpose vehicle (SPV) and the implementation of funding. The investment per person can be up to $1,000. The amount of the total investment varies from case to case. In this case, most leads to investors come from the startups themselves. So far, Cartooli has invested in one Georgian startup and is working with up to 10 other startups to facilitate the funding round. Startups can fill out a request form online.

continued on next page

Appendix 4 *continued*

No.	Name	Description
4	**Catapult Georgia**	Catapult VC, a California-based company that invests in technology companies, is launching a fund to invest in innovative startups in Georgia. Officially called Catapult Georgia I, LP, the fund aims to raise $50 million. It will collaborate with the United States (US) Market Access Center and Startup Grind Tbilisi to provide capital and mentorship to about 50 Georgian startups over the next decade. The fund has been in the fundraising phase since 2021 and has not yet made any investments.
5	**Georgia Capital**	Georgia Capital is very established and one of the largest investment funds in Georgia. It is listed on the London Stock Exchange. The company makes substantial investments in traditional manufacturing and service industries, including the banking sector. The total value of Georgia Capital's portfolio is GEL3.6 billion. To fund and support technology startups, the firm has committed $3.2 million to Redberry Startup Studio to support technology startups through direct equity investments and an incubator program. The entire process goes through Redberry. There are no open channels for startups to apply for funding. Startup Studio's most common approach is to identify early-stage entrepreneurs and seek opportunities to become cofounders of the startup.
6	**Georgian Venture Capital Association**	The Georgian Venture Capital Association (GVCA) was established in 2017. Its mission is to promote the development and consolidation of the venture capital and private equity sector in Georgia by creating a favorable investment climate, establishing a legal framework for venture capital, promoting the culture of entrepreneurship, supporting seed-stage start-ups, and bridging the gap between Georgian and international investors. There are no data available on how many startups have been supported by the GVCA and what amounts have been invested. Currently, the GVCA is not the most active stakeholder of the ecosystem. The gvca.ge website contains a general inquiry form for potential members or other interested startups.
7	**Global Startup Foundation**	The Global Startup Foundation was established in 2019 by the Business and Technology University with the support of Georgia's Innovation and Technology Agency (GITA), Israel's Silicon Wadi, and Israeli Techub in Georgia. The foundation organizes annual pitching events for Georgian–Israeli investors, for which startups can apply publicly. About 10 selected startups are invited to pitch. The startups that have investors' interest are invited for further discussions with investors. So far, one startup has been funded: Echolize is an influencer marketing tool for businesses. In addition to the equity investment, the startup was able to receive a matching amount from GITA's equity-free grant, totaling up to GEL1,300,000 from both sources.

continued on next page

Appendix 4 *continued*

No.	Name	Description
8	**Isari Ventures**	Isari Ventures was launched in October 2022 and will invest in smart, creative, and resilient Georgian founders who are operating at a pre-product market-fit stage. It has already invested in Phubber (online fashion retailer), Omofox (digital freight forwarder) and Kernel (digital accounting tools for SMEs). It has $5 million to invest in the coming years.
9	**Mission Gate**	Mission Gate is a San Francisco-based venture capital firm founded in 2014 by professionals from Georgia. Mission Gate aims to invest in seed and early-stage startups in fintech, consumer technology, blockchain, and digital health. Their website lists 15 startups in their portfolio, including several from Georgia. In addition to investments, they provide relevant connections and advice to startups at various stages of growth. There is no indication of the amount of investments available and there is no active and public outreach to startups in Georgia yet. Most partnerships seem to come through leads and personal connections.
10	**TECH Friends of Georgia**	TECH Friends of Georgia brings together US-based angel investors to support technology startups in Georgia. The initiative works with the Government of Georgia through GITA. As part of the collaboration, GITA will help identify local startups with global potential that will receive international experience, contacts with California-based startups and access to up to $500,000. The initiative is still in its early stages, no deals have been closed, and investor recruitment and fund building are ongoing.

Source: Authors, based on interviews, desk research, and data from official websites.

Appendix 5: Supportive Spaces and Community Initiatives for Startups in Georgia

No.	Name	Type	Scope
1	**TechParks**	Government	TechParks provides the largest government-built and managed innovation spaces for coworking and co-creation, and also hosts different events and workshops. Currently, there are TechParks in Tbilisi, Batumi, Zugdidi, Telavi, Kaspi, Gurjanii, Akhmeta, and Ozurgeti.
2	**FabLabs**	Government/University-based	Fabrication laboratories (FabLabs) are government-initiated spaces in TechParks, public universities, or other spaces where citizens can use different equipment and devices such as 3D printers, scanners, and other smart devices for quick prototyping.
3	**Innovation Centers**	Government	More than five innovation centers have been established in local municipalities based in libraries and other municipal spaces. The centers serve as a base to host various workshops and training to introduce digital technologies to the local, mostly rural population.
4	**Spark Incubator**	Government	A European Union-supported incubator program of Tbilisi City Hall, the incubator provides space for interactions, workshops, training, and mentoring.
5	**Rustavi Innovation Lab**	Nonprofit, initially supported by the government	Established by Rustavi City Hall with support from UNDP, the hub is focused on finding innovative solutions to the city's problems. The hub supports entrepreneurial education, intersectoral collaboration, youth employment, and municipal service development.
6	**GeoLab**	University-based	GeoLab is the result of a public–private partnership between GITA, Georgian American University, a digital-service company Leavingstone, and a mobile operator Geocell. The lab offers coworking spaces and paid courses for the development of IT skills, as well as nonprofit programs to promote the spread of digital skills, especially among vulnerable groups.
7	**UniLab**	University-based	UniLab is located at Ilia Chavchavadze State University. It offers students short-term courses in graphic design, web development, and project management.
8	**UG Startup Factory**	University-based	UG Startup Factory is based at the University of Georgia and offers students an intensive startup acceleration program, mentorship, and potential small-scale funding, training, and development.
9	**C10**	University-based	C10 is a startup accelerator for students at Caucasus University. It offers students various guest lectures, hackathons, and other activities to enhance entrepreneurial education and support startup creation.

continued on next page

Appendix 5 *continued*

No.	Name	Type	Scope
10	**BTU Entrepreneurship Center**	University-based	Business and Technology University established the Center for Entrepreneurship in partnership with the world-leading Henley Center for Entrepreneurship. The main goal of the center is to significantly contribute to the development and internationalization of Georgia's entrepreneurship ecosystem. The center aims to achieve this through continuous research in this field, initiating discussions among ecosystem stakeholders on the necessary improvements to the legal framework, proposing innovative solutions and projects, etc. BTU is the first Georgian university to become a member of Massachusetts Institute of Technology's innovative startup network.
11	**TSU Knowledge Transfer and Innovation Center**	University-based	The Knowledge Transfer and Innovation Center was established at Ivane Javakhishvili Tbilisi State University to serve two main functions: (i) support knowledge transfer activities, such as a unified university approach to intellectual property commercialization; and (ii) enhance the entrepreneurial ecosystem at the university by improving support facilities and establishing startup processes, such as FabLab and accelerator programs.
12	**Impact Hub Tbilisi**	Private	Impact Hub Tbilisi is a local representative of a global network. It offers coworking space, training, workshops, hackathons, and pre-accelerator programs. The hub is one of the major supporters of social innovation and co-creation.
13	**Startup Grind**	Private	Startup Grind is a global startup community designed to educate, inspire, and connect entrepreneurs. The Georgia chapter promotes entrepreneurial knowledge sharing by organizing events and conferences and providing international networking spaces for Georgian entrepreneurs.
14	**Future Laboratory**	Private	Future Laboratory is an innovation consulting and management company that focuses primarily on integrating technology, project-based learning, and innovation infrastructure into learning at private schools in Tbilisi. In addition, the team provides assistance for entrepreneurship and accelerator programs for students.
15	**Startup Büro**	Private	Startup Büro works closely with the private and public sectors to design and implement hackathons, business bootcamps, incubation, pre-acceleration and acceleration programs, community meetings, training, and conferences, and other skill- and capacity-building programs for entrepreneurs, innovators, and creatives.
16	**TBC Startuper**	Private	Startuper is a program of TBC Bank that aims to stimulate new businesses and promote the development of startups. The program includes financial and nonfinancial support for startups, including startup loans, training, individual consultations, media support, and events and conferences.

continued on next page

Appendix 5 *continued*

No.	Name	Type	Scope
17	**Startup Info**	Virtual Community	Startup Info is an online community on Facebook that brings together more than 10,000 members who are startup founders, ecosystem players, or those interested in entrepreneurial development. The space is moderated to provide educational resources, share information about interesting events in the ecosystem, and host Q&As.

Source: Authors, based on interviews and data from official websites.

Appendix 6: Selection of Information Technology and Engineering Training Courses at Georgian Educational Institutions and Training Centers

Name of Institution	Type	Courses Offered (Related to Information Technology and Engineering)
Ivane Javakhishvili Tbilisi State University	Public University	Academic programs: BA and MA Mathematics, Computer Science, Electronic and Electric Engineering, Information Systems
Georgian Technical University	Public University	Academic programs: BA and MA in Business Technology, Informatics and Control Systems, Telecommunication, Civil Engineering
Ilia State University	Public University	Academic programs: BA in Mathematics, Computer Engineering, Computer Science, Civil Engineering, Electronic and Electric Engineering; MA in Software Engineering, Mathematics
Akaki Tsereteli State University	Public University	Academic programs: BA and MA degrees in Electrical Engineering, Computer Science, Mathematics, BioTech; MA in Computer Science, Mathematics
Batumi Shota Rustaveli State University	Public University	Academic programs: BA in Computer Science, Mathematics; MA in Computer Science, Mathematics Vocational Education: IT Systems Support
Free University	Private University	Academic programs: BA in Mathematics and Computer Science, Electrical and Computer Engineering Marketing
Business and Technology University	Private University	Academic programs: BA in Information Technologies, Digital Marketing; MA in Information Systems Management – DevOps, Business Administration and Modern Technologies; Short-term courses and training programs (e.g., Mobile and Web development, Coding School for Women)
Caucasus University	Private University	Academic programs: BA in Computer Science, Electronics and Computer Engineering, Graphic Design; MA in Information Technology Management
Kutaisi International University	Private University	Academic programs: BA in Computer Science, Mathematics, Management; MSc in Finance and Information Management
San Diego State University	Public–Private Partnership with Universities	Academic programs: BA in Computer Science, Computer Engineering, Electrical Engineering, Civil Engineering, Biochemistry/Chemistry
GITA training through TechParks, Innovation Centers and Fablabs	Government	Different government educational programs and short-term training in Computer Programming, Software Development, No-Code Development Platforms, UX/UI Design, Industrial Design, 2D/3D Modeling, Electronic Engineering, Robotics, Computer Science, Artificial Intelligence, Front-End and Back-End Development, Cybersecurity, Blockchain, Mobile and Game Development, DevOps, QA Engineering, Cloud Services

continued on next page

Appendix 6 *continued*

Name of Institution	Type	Courses Offered (Related to Information Technology and Engineering)
GeoLab	Private Training Center	Short- to long-term courses in Web Development (HTML, CSS, PHP, Wordpress, Drupal, React, JavaScript), Mobile Development (iOS, Java, Android), Gaming (Unity), Programming (C#, Python, Oracle Development), and UI/UX and graphic design
IT Academy Step	Private Training Center	6-month to 1.5-year training programs in Networks and Cybersecurity, Graphic Design, Front-End Development, UI/UX Design, IT support
Smart Academy	Private Training Center	32 lecture/hour training courses in Front-End Development, Mobile Development (IOS, Android), Python, UI/UX, C#, Motion Graphics, Cloud services
TBC IT Academy	Private Training Center	2- to 6-month training programs in Mobile Development (Android, IoS), DevOps, Test Automation, Full Stack Development, Backend Development, Front-End Development, UI/UX
Tbilisi School of Communication	Private Training Center	14–32 lecture training programs including on Data Science, Front-End Development, Android Development, Angular, Flutter, React, UX Research and Design
Academy of Digital Industries	Private Training Center	Up to 2 months professional training courses on UI and UX Design, Frontend (HTML & CSS), Wordpress, JavaScript and Angular, PHP, React, Linux, Web Development, JAVA, Motion Design
Digital Bus	Private Training Center	6-week to 6-month training programs on Frond-End fundamentals, C#, UI/UX Design, Graphic Design, Motion Design, Python, Robotics
Information Technologies Academy	Public Vocational Educational Training College	The oldest specialized vocational training center, established in 2007. Offering short-term training courses and full vocational education courses on Computer Networks Administration (Cisco), Web Technologies, PHP Development, C# programming, Python, Java, Graphic Design, Information Technologies
BitCamp	Private Training Center	Started as the country's largest tech-education Facebook group (43,000 members), BitCamp is run by local senior software engineers and provides training courses, mentoring and employment opportunities for those interested to switch careers or start a new profession. Training is offered in front-end and back-end software development.

Source: Authors, based on interviews, desk research, and data from official websites.

References

ACT Research. 2011. *Saving Behavior Assessment Survey in Georgia: Report on Quantitative Survey*. Tbilisi.

Agenda.GE. 2022. Rakuten Viber Opens Tbilisi Office for Mobile Application Development.

Business Media Georgia. 2021. It Is Wrong to Ask Companies to Pay Taxes with a Back Date – Papiashvili on the Entities in the Virtual Zone (in Georgian). Tbilisi.

Caucasus Business Week (CBW). 2019. Digital Agency Redberry Attracted 3.2 Million USD Investment from Georgian Capital. Tbilisi.

European Bank for Reconstruction and Development (EBRD). 2017. Business Environment and Enterprise Performance Survey 2017. London.

EU4Business. 2020. Results 2020: Number of SMEs Supported per Access to Finance Instruments in Eastern Partnership.

Global Entrepreneurship Monitor (GEM). 2014. *Women Entrepreneurship in Georgia*.

_____. 2016. Entrepreneurial Behaviour and Attitudes.

Government of Georgia. 2020. Ordinance No. 619 On Determining the Status of an International Company and Approving the List of Permitted Activities and Certain Expenses. Enacted 8 October 2020. Tbilisi.

Heritage Foundation. 2021. Index of Economic Freedom 2021. Washington, DC.

Investor.ge. 2021a. $50 Million for Georgian Startups – Catapult VC Fund Puts Boots on the Ground in Tbilisi. Tbilisi.

_____. 2021b. Pulsar AI: Startup Dreams Come True with Georgia's First Startup Exit. Tbilisi.

Legislative Herald of Georgia. 2006. Law of Georgia on Promotion and Guarantees of Investment Activity. Enacted 30 June 2006. Tbilisi.

_____. 2020. Law of Georgia on Investment of Funds. Issued 14 July 2020. Tbilisi.

Murmann, M. 2017. The Startups Most Likely to Succeed Have Technical Founders Who Quickly Hire Businesspeople. *Harvard Business Review*.

National Statistics Office of Georgia (GEOSTAT). 2014. 2014 General Population Census Results. Tbilisi.

_____. 2020. Indicators of Using Information and Communication Technologies (ICT) in Household 2020. Tbilisi.

Organisation for Economic Co-operation and Development (OECD). 2018. Programme for International Student Assessment (PISA): Results from PISA 2018. Country Note. Paris.

_____. 2019. OECD Reviews of Evaluation and Assessment in Education: Georgia. Paris.

Startup Genome. 2019. *Global Startup Ecosystem Report 2019. Startup Ecosystem Lifecycle*.

_____. 2020. *The Global Startup Ecosystem Report 2020*.

_____. 2022. *Global Startup Ecosystem Report: Cleantech Edition*.

StartupBlink. 2022. Global Startup Ecosystem Index 2022

Statista. 2022. Projected Global Digital Health Market Size from 2019 to 2025.

TBC. 2021. *TBC Group Sustainability Report 2021*.

Transparency International. 2020. *Corruption Perceptions Index 2019*.

Transparency International Georgia. 2020. Trends in Georgia's Agriculture Sector in 2012–2019. Tbilisi.

United Nations Economic Commission for Europe (UNECE). 2020. *Innovation for Sustainable Development: Review of Georgia*. New York.

USAID Georgia. 2017. *Innovation and Technology in Georgia: Annual Report: 2017*. Tbilisi.

World Bank. 2019. *Enterprise Surveys: Georgia 2019 Profile*. Washington, DC.

_____. 2020a. *Doing Business 2020: Comparing Business Regulation in 190 Economies*. Washington, DC.

_____. 2020b. *The Human Capital Index 2020 Update: Human Capital in the Time of COVID-19*. Washington, DC.

World Economic Forum (WEF). 2019. *The Global Competitiveness Report 2019*. Geneva.

* 9 7 8 9 2 9 2 7 0 0 3 6 2 *